Set Apart
for God

To
Dearest Joy.

May God Bless you
as you read this !!
Thanks for your
help, love e support
love
Rosie

Set Apart for God

The Call to a Surrendered Life

John Mulinde

Sovereign World

Sovereign World Ltd
PO Box 777
Tonbridge
Kent TN11 0ZS
England

ISBN 1-85240-430-2

Cover design by CCD, www.ccdgroup.co.uk
Typeset by CRB Associates, Reepham, Norfolk
Printed in the United States of America

Contents

Acknowledgements   7

Foreword by Charlie Cleverley   9

PART 1: The Call of the Hour

Chapter 1   The Call of the Hour   12

Chapter 2   Sowing for Victory   31

Chapter 3   Set Apart: Bible Examples   37

Chapter 4   Idols of the Heart   49

Chapter 5   Nazirites   71

Chapter 6   Procrastination and Distractions   77

Chapter 7   Prison Gates   82

PART 2: The Process

Chapter 8   Surrender: The Starting Point   96

Chapter 9   Redeeming the Time   107

Chapter 10   True Worship   114

Chapter 11   A People of the Word   119

Chapter 12   Responding to the Call   123

Resources   128

Acknowledgements

This book is based on teaching I gave during the AfriCamp 2002, when I shared from my heart how the Lord had intervened in my life with a call to be *Set Apart for Him*, and the things I have experienced since that time.

Special appreciation goes to George Otis Jr and his wife Lisa, who encouraged us by the recognition they gave to God's work in our country. George and Lisa travelled to Uganda with their film crew to document the extent of God's transformation of our country. They then made a record of this testimony for all the world to see in the *Transformations II* video. Not only did this inspire the pastors, intercessors and people of Uganda, but it also gave us the push we so needed to keep us going strong and undistracted in our labour for the further changes which God has promised.

I also acknowledge the faithfulness of my team in World Trumpet Mission and all the various volunteers who selflessly give themselves to serve with me in very trying circumstances. We have accomplished much together. I have no doubt at all that our work has been able to reach this point where it is touching nations worldwide only because of this dedicated teamwork. God bless each one of you.

I particularly want to acknowledge all the technical assistance from Lily Mudasia who compiled the book, Stephanie Powers and the many other professional people who have helped put it together. This includes both those in Uganda and those further afield who made invaluable contributions. God bless you, dear ones.

Lastly, I would like to dedicate this book from the bottom of my heart to my family, especially my dear children, who have sacrificed so much to allow me the time to write and travel widely when they so needed my company. Your sacrifice meant even more to me because it was made at a time when there was no one to be Mama to you. I have learnt a lot from your patience, understanding and unconditional love. Thank you, Hope, Geoffrey, Jackson, Abraham, Gideon, Emmanuel, and little Angel. May you share doubly from the blessing that will come as lives are changed by this book. I love you dearly. Shalom!

At the release of this edition, I would like to recognise the loving support and partnership of Sheila Mulinde, my wife and best friend. May God richly bless you for always being there for me. My love for you grows each day.

Finally, I thank You, God the Father, the Son and the Holy Spirit, for without You I can do nothing.

John Mulinde

Foreword

John is a man of prayer and a motivator for prayer. His is a cry 'from another country' to seek the face of God. With a whip of rope Jesus cleansed the temple and called her back to being a House of Prayer for all nations. John is one who has secured a whole mountain just outside Kampala to become that house of prayer. There may not be many buildings, but there is certainly prayer: unceasing, persistent, united, penetrative, desperate prayer. The prayer that takes hold of God and 'will not let Him go'. And the nation of Uganda, the pearl of Africa, has been brought back from the brink of disaster, through prayer. This book contains vital, motivating, prophetic teaching, applicable to individuals, families, churches and nations that we cannot afford to miss. I and Anita have known John for nearly ten years. I have been present at different family milestones and he has deeply impacted our lives and those of our children. He has been a friend as well as a constant challenge. I thank God for bringing him to us for such a time as this.

The dynamite that is contained between the covers of this book is a result of a time of seeking God at the same period as the attacks on the World Trade Center of 9/11. The first time I heard John preach these messages, at Trumpet Center in the heart of Kampala, I remember being deeply stirred. I believe that this call to be 'set apart for God' is something that the Holy Spirit is saying persistently to the Church today. It has to do with the call to be a passionate, forerunner Church that prepares the way of the Lord. It is linked to the call to be a lovesick Bride of Christ who will put seeking the presence of Christ above the programmes that drive us. It has to do with the passion and courage of the martyrs that shapes nations.

I believe in strategy, and so does John. I believe that we need to see in the West every Christian an intercessor, in every home a prayer altar, every church become a house of prayer and in every town a city-wide prayer centre. But before all these, we need people set apart. As John says, most people opt for strategies, methods or formulae, rather than allow God to deal with their own hearts.

John is a voice in the wilderness calling for the preparation of the heart that is the preparation of the way of the Lord.

Mike Bickle has said: 'Something is on the horizon for planet earth for which the Church is completely unprepared. An unprepared Church cannot possibly prepare an unprepared world.'[1] I believe this key book is part of the preparing of the people today. May God lead you to Him as you read, mark and inwardly digest it. May it come like a trumpet call to be set apart for Him.

Charlie Cleverly
St Aldate's Church, Oxford
May 2005

Note
1. Mike Bickle, *The Pleasures of Loving God* (Charisma House, 2000), p. 73.

PART 1

The Call of the Hour

Chapter 1

The Call of the Hour

The night of 10 September 2001 will remain stamped on my memory forever. That night, during my time of prayer, the Lord spoke words to me that were destined to change my life and ministry radically. That change has started, and only God knows how far it will go, or how long this period of strict discipline will take. But I dare to say already that the difficulty and challenges of the journey are well worth it.

I was in the city of Seattle in the United States of America at the invitation of my dear friend George Otis Jr, the producer of the well-known *Transformations* videos. The videos are recordings of how communities all over the world are being transformed by the power of God. Millions of copies of the videos have been distributed worldwide.

Testimonies abound of how the videos have created spiritual hunger in people from all walks of life, inspiring them to seek God more, individually as well as corporately. Christians worldwide are coming to appreciate the power of prayer and of working in unity, and a determination to bring about community transformation is sweeping through churches everywhere.

I had travelled to Seattle to make a recording which, along with others, was going to be used in a follow-up to the *Transformations II* video. George Otis had invited several leaders from across the world, who had been part of the process of God transforming their communities, to share the lessons and core values they had learnt. His desire was to build a body of *core values* that are evident in each case of transformation, which could be of help to those in other communities who are hungry to see transformation. It was hoped that, as intercessors studied and pursued these core values, God would honour their faith and guide them into strategies that would transform their own communities. This is a cause that I also fully believe in. I am sure it is God-inspired, and I would give everything and anything to see it succeed.

I arrived in Seattle on 8 September 2001 and began to prepare myself for the recording on the 11th. On the night of 10 September, I was praying and interceding for the following day's programme when a heavy burden came upon my heart. It suddenly dawned upon me that we were actually taking an immense responsibility upon ourselves. I became aware that there are millions of God's people who have watched the *Transformations* videos, and many more who will watch them in the future, whose sole cry is, 'For the sake of our cities and nations, just show us how to do it and we will go for it, whatever the cost!' These are people who would do anything to see similar results in their own communities. All they need is some clear guidance as to how to go about it.

On the one hand, my heart felt extremely excited about this opportunity. Without a doubt the core values, shared as they are by people with first-hand experience from various transformed communities, would be a great and invaluable treasure. But on the other hand, I realised that *if the right state of heart were not attained by the seekers*, and if the seekers did not see their own part in the *sickness* of their lands causing them to cry out for the healing to start with them, there would never be power to change their lands for God. They could be presented with all the principles of transformation, and they might even implement them zealously, yet still see no results. Very often, because people are seeking a quick solution they miss the most obvious thing: they ignore the basic work of brokenness, total surrender to God and a rejection of the status quo.

I am convinced that communities are transformed when a few people in them reach a point of yearning for God so desperately that they will pay any price to see His intervention in the land. This is the same holy desperation that has driven all past revivalists in church history the world over. Experience shows, however, that most people today opt for the strategies, methods or formulae which they believe will produce certain spiritual experiences, rather than allow God to deal with their own hearts first in such a way as to equip them to impact their worlds with their lives. Therefore, as I pondered this reality the burden on my heart was: how do we move God's people beyond concentrating on methods alone to focus instead on experiencing real *personal transformation from the inside out* that would progress from the individual to the community? I felt certain that this was the cry of God's heart: to bring people to a place of dynamic encounter with Him so that He could work powerfully through them to change their nations.

I hope I will not be misunderstood as seeking in any way to undermine the sharing of lessons learnt in past transformations. I would be the last person to do that, for that would be the same as denying myself. My whole life and ministry is a product of this very phenomenon: God intervening in the affairs of His people in a modern nation state.

Yet I had within me a deep fear: What if, even after people have embraced the values we share, they still did not see breakthrough in their communities – because they have ignored the work *necessary within their own hearts*? What about those who have tried every strategy and pattern they have heard about and have now become weary? They would not be keen on trying anything new, or stretching their faith any further! They need to know why, after all these years of effort, they now find themselves facing an impasse.

World Scepticism

Knowing the sceptics of this present world, and the speed with which theologians and scholars rush to discredit everyone and everything at the slightest provocation, I felt really jealous for the noble cause we had come to Seattle to work for. I did not want this work to be ridiculed in any way or to come to naught. I desired with all my heart to see it accomplish its intended purpose. Yet I did not know what to do or how we could avoid what I was fearing. So I cried out the more to God, 'Lord, You know our hearts. You know that all we desire is to see You glorified throughout the earth. Please guide this whole process to produce what will make Your heart rejoice in Your people in the nations.'

I felt strongly in my heart that what God had begun to do through George Otis Jr was intended to inspire such faith in God's people worldwide that they would break age-old strongholds over their nations and cities, and this would open the door for God-glorifying revivals throughout the world. I felt an undeniable conviction that not only is this dream possible but that *this is actually the ordained hour for it to happen.*

(Please note that at the time I was pondering these issues, I had not heard what the other speakers who had been invited to the core values' recording would be sharing. I believe that this was just God's way of drawing my attention to something bigger than what I had come to do in Seattle and setting my feet on a journey that has come to mean so much to me and countless others.)

Strongholds in the Nations

As I continued in my prayer and travail, I reflected on the nations to which I had travelled in Africa, Europe, the Americas, the Middle East, the Far East and other parts of the world. There is no denying that some real awakening is going on in all of these regions. There is undeniably an increased volume of prayer and more and more people are becoming hungry for God. People are becoming increasingly aware that God requires them to step into *deeper waters*. The reason I felt so desperate was not because I was not seeing any results in my own ministry in these nations. On the contrary, a lot has happened beyond even my own expectations.

However, I could also see in my spirit that there are strongholds deeply and manifestly entrenched in the lifestyles of people in every region of the world. These are so deeply rooted that it appears almost impossible to bring communities to the point where they can experience God's glorious power of revival. There are so many things that stand in the way of genuine nation-sweeping revivals, such as culture, tradition, mindsets, indulgent lifestyles and the general world view of people today. I was profoundly aware of how the nations, and their peoples – including even the Christian believers – are held in captivity to their social systems. These bondages have become so much a part of us that we scarcely notice how they cause our lives to *differ from what is in the Word of God. Instead, we conform to the world around us.*

When I compared the extent of the revival that I sensed in the Spirit waiting to be poured out over the nations, and what was practically happening on the ground all over the world, I was left with no doubt at all in my mind that there is need for a major break from our present trend, if we are going to see God's glory cover the nations. For example, in **Europe**, as we minister there, trying to share from the practical lessons of transformation that God has graciously taught us in Uganda (things God Himself has sent us out to go and share worldwide saying, *'Freely you have received, freely give'*, Matthew 10:8), we are always coming up against 'the system', and we often hear these words from well-meaning people: 'You can't do that here. It won't work here because *this is Europe'*, and 'You don't expect that to happen in Europe, do you?'

In **Africa**, in spite of all the wonderful stories of God moving in various nations and regions, we cannot fail to see the power of spiritual bondage all over the continent, and this also includes my native Uganda. Time and time again you come up against the same brick wall; it may manifest itself in different ways, but the message is always the same: you cannot change things for God beyond what the system will allow. God can only go so far and no further! *There is always a point beyond which people think it becomes irrelevant even to consider applying God to the real-life issues that affect people.*

In the **Middle East** you have to be even more careful. Nowhere does my heart ache as it does when I am in Israel or the Arab world. As I minister there, I am always struck by how God's heart is breaking for His people, and how His love is reaching out to them, both Jew and Arab, but Oh! the forces at work are so great! When I speak in Israel or in the Arab world, I must always be extra prayerful and seek God to help me tread lightly. The air is always so tense with the many different currents that operate in the region, and yet it is not always possible to 'stroke people's backs', when I have to get across a prophetic word. Sometimes the truth hurts! Not every pill can be sweet! On occasions we have to put our lives on the line to obey God! Nevertheless, as we lift our eyes in the spirit and still behold the impregnable wall of spiritual blindness and resistance, we wonder, 'Oh God, how and when will this wall ever come down?'

In **North America**, **South America**, in the **Far East** and **in every land and nation**, the world system seems to have locked God's people within a certain mould of spiritual limitation. Political, social, economic, cultural and spiritual forces all seem to work together to convince the people that it is unpractical to expect any more from God. I suddenly felt heavily weighed down by the realisation that in every region, whether it be in Europe or Africa, America or Asia, and even in communities where a degree of transformation has already occurred such as in Guatemala or Uganda, the world system has such a strong hold on God's people that the Church has come to adjust its expectations to only what seems *possible within the system.*

As the Word is being ministered, preachers labour so hard to fit *within the system*, that what ends up being released is often so watered down that it loses the impact needed to change our world. Doctrines have been created to explain it all away and make God's people feel comfortable in this mediocrity. A subtle veil is separating today's Church from the fullness of its divine inheritance here on earth.

As a result, this latter House of God is only a shadow of the former House seen in the first century. Many have even come to accept and believe that this is all that can be expected from God today, but no one who has ever gazed on the face of the Lord would settle for such a conclusion! We know that His heart is craving to do much more for the human race than anything we have witnessed so far. It is prophesied that an end-time worldwide revival will occur in *all nations* that will surpass the glory of the first works, and for sure this must happen. It does not matter how impossible it may appear! It has to happen!

Suddenly, as these thoughts raced through my mind on that night in Seattle, it struck my heart that there was something God was trying to open my eyes to see. If the prophecy of God's end-time revival is to come true and if the knowledge of God's glory is to cover the earth as the waters cover the sea, then there must be a way around all these obstacles we see in the nations. *I began to search for the key that would unlock the door of nations and cities* to allow God to invade today's world with His glorious transforming power. My mind raced back through the pages of the Bible to seek for answers. I was strongly impressed by stories of God breaking seemingly impossible systems in history to transform nations and communities in such a way that whole empires bowed down in acknowledgement of His name.

Old Testament Examples

It happened with Moses when he confronted Pharaoh's Egypt to secure the Hebrews' release and a whole nation was redeemed from a *seemingly impenetrable system*. It happened with Samuel, when, in a time of great spiritual barrenness,

Israel as a nation experienced revival and transformation. A land in which the Word of God was scarce and in which there was no one with a vision was suddenly filled with the Word of God and all nations knew about it. It happened with Daniel, Meshach, Shadrach and Abednego in Babylon. There, the supreme rulers declared openly, on several different occasions, that there is no God like the God of Israel, and that all people in the empire should honour Him. God even intervened in the life of Nebuchadnezzar to the point of breaking his pride and causing him to acknowledge His name. And this is still the same God we serve! It happened in the days of King Josiah and of the prophets Elijah, Jeremiah and John the Baptist. As these stories streamed through my mind my heart began to race. Yes! I knew without a doubt that the Spirit of God was leading me to discover a gem I had never touched before, something that might unlock the door to the transformation of nations worldwide. Faced with our world system today there seems to be no hope of turning whole nations to God. But is that not how it must also have appeared in the days of Moses and of Daniel, and in the days of Samuel and of Elijah?

New Testament Examples

Let us turn our attention to the apostles as they started out to fulfil the Great Commission. Let us take a moment to consider the challenges facing the early Church in those days. They lived in a system deeply entrenched in religious beliefs, which had been developed through the nation's history of God's dealings with them over centuries, actually millennia:

- They had the law, received supernaturally by Moses on the mountain
- They had the prophets who under the Holy Spirit had dealt so powerfully with their forefathers
- They had a history rich with examples of God's miracles both in their own land and in foreign lands.

These were the foundation blocks of their beliefs, formed out of thousands of years of documented evidence that God was undeniably and vividly involved in it all.

But it was to these very people that the apostles had to take the gospel message, proclaiming that there was no true salvation in all the age-old beliefs they trusted in, that no one would ever see God unless they put their faith in a little-known, rather unconventional, self-proclaimed prophet called Jesus. The apostles had to convince the Jews that this same Jesus, who had lived among them only a short while ago, was truly the long-awaited Messiah of the Jews; that He had indeed ushered in God's New Testament which in effect had done away with the Old; that He was the King of the Jews who came in the line of David, the Judge of all the world, the embodiment of everything the prophets had ever prophesied!

And as if that were not enough, they had to convince the Jews that this Jesus was actually the Son of God, literally equal to God Himself; that He existed in the beginning before the creation of anything; that He was with God, and is actually God Himself; that He is the Author of all things and without Him nothing was made that was made. All this they had to convince the Jews who had known their God for thousands of years under different terms. Wow! Now think about that for a challenging task!

Forgive me, dear reader, for putting it so bluntly, but this is how it must have appeared in many Jewish minds. Surely, the idea that eternal life could only be found in the Nazarene, who had just been killed openly and publicly as a criminal in Jerusalem, was no more appealing to the people of that day than our claims about Jesus are to our world today? But the apostles went forth in the power of the Lord and successfully proclaimed the Good News to their generation. Who can deny that they made a life-changing impact everywhere they went?

Consider Paul and the other evangelists who went throughout the pagan nations preaching the gospel of Jesus Christ to people who had traditionally worshipped everything but the God of Israel since time immemorial. Remember that Israel, as a nation, was under Roman rule, both militarily and politically. Culturally and intellectually they were under the shadow of the Greeks. Religiously they were often ridiculed because, unlike other nations who were rich in many gods (a god for every need), the Israelites had only one God to whom they turned for everything – and at that time He did not even appear to be doing very much for them as regards their shame under foreign domination. In all senses the Israelites were underdogs who stood to be pitied by those who considered themselves 'much more civilised peoples' (see, for example, Acts 17:16–25, 30–32). And yet it was to these same people that Jesus gave the mandate of the Great Commission: *'Go therefore and make disciples of all the nations'* (Matthew 28:19).

Never before in all history had anyone attempted to bring the peoples of the nations, with all their diversity of cultures and beliefs, to believe in one God. But this is what Jesus was demanding of His followers: *'Go therefore and make disciples of all nations ... teaching them to observe all things that I have commanded you.'* Some of these nations were richer, stronger, more civilised and more enlightened than Israel was perceived to be. Others were purely barbaric, deeply entrenched in satanic worship, idolatry and even human sacrifice, which their forefathers had practised over many generations. The apostles were commissioned to go to these nations and convince them that they needed to change their beliefs, break out of their traditional world systems and lifestyles, and put their faith in the one Lord called Jesus Christ, King of the Jews. And if they would do that, all their sins would be forgiven and they would inherit eternal life! This same Jesus who had died and rose from the dead would come back and take them to heaven to live with Him in glory forever and ever. How about that for a challenge!

Compare their task with ours today. Without a doubt, theirs was as impossible a task as any we could cite today! And yet the most amazing thing about the early Church is the degree of success they experienced in turning nations upside down for Jesus. Despite all the odds against them, the early Church took the gospel with power. They broke through barriers and systems and brought people to Jesus with incredible results. Nations of totally heathen people were radically changed as they were penetrated with the gospel. Age-old traditions were dismantled, customs abandoned and religions discarded. In some cases even whole economic systems collapsed as people turned away from idolatry and the trade that depended on it (e.g. Acts 19:18–19, 23–34). The apostles made such an impact on their world that the unbelievers of their day testified about them saying: *'These who have turned the world upside down have come here too'* (Acts 17:6). We should believe that if they did it then, we too can do it in our day. YES! We can transform our nation for Christ today just as they did two thousand years ago. After all we serve the same Lord and have the same Great Commission.

But Why Is It not Happening?

Is it that the Church today does not have the same anointing as the early Church? I would be the last to believe that. The same Holy Spirit they had is the very one we also have today. So as I pondered these things that night in Seattle, I cried out the more that God would show me the key our forerunners had which we are missing today. I was on my face before the Lord a good part of that night, pouring out my heart in anguish.

'Lord,' I cried out to Him, 'what is it that has weakened the Church of our day so much? We don't even seem to be bothered by the growing moral decay of our day! What must we do to break the power of wickedness that is holding the nations in such a vicious grip? Is there no way to bring spiritual liberation to the people of our day? Lord, are You not the same God who worked with the early Church to break the same powers over whole nations? Could You have done that yesterday and yet not be willing to do the same today? But, Lord, You are no respecter of persons, and the Great Commission You gave to them is the very same Commission You give to us. The same promise You spoke to them in

Matthew 28:20 still applies in our day: *"and lo, I am with you always, even to the end of the age."*

'Lord, You prayed for us as much as for them, *"As You sent Me into the world, I also have sent them into the world ... I do not pray for these alone, but also for those who will believe in Me through their word"* [John 17:17, 20]. Moreover You promised in Your Word that *"The glory of this latter house shall be greater than of the former"* [Haggai 2:9 KJV]. And again You said, *"For the earth will be filled with the knowledge of the glory of the LORD, As the waters cover the sea"* [Habakkuk 2:14]. Father, are we wrong to believe You for greater works in our day than those You accomplished in the first century? Surely what we are seeing today is a far cry from what they witnessed in the first century. Lord, please give Your servant the revelation I am crying out for. What was the early Church's secret, and how can we rediscover it?'

This was the gist of my heart cry, as I pleaded before the Lord. The pressure of knowing that the next day I was going to do a recording sharing lessons learnt in community transformation weighed heavily on my heart. I had been asked to talk about the role of prayer in community transformation. I knew that the values I have learnt are gems in kingdom-building. I knew also that what the other speakers had already shared from their own experience was invaluable. Nevertheless, there was no doubt in my heart that I was being invited by the Holy Spirit to explore an area whose significance reached far beyond what I would need for the following morning's recording. I felt a burning conviction deep in my heart that, if I followed the leading I was sensing, I was about to embark on something that would change my entire approach to ministry and maybe even my whole life. I did not have the slightest idea about what was coming my way.

The Lord Answers

As I pondered these facts the Spirit of the Lord began to pour His word into my heart. It came as burning fire blazing through my heart, strong and clear. I have tried as best as I can to put it into words:

> 'Understand that the world and its systems have been changing and will continue to change. New developments are affecting the way nations are acting concerning their destinies, and the way their peoples are responding to God. But besides all that, you need to understand at this very moment that there is going to be a major shift in the heavenlies. The *powers in the heavenlies over the entire world are going to shift irreversibly.* And this is going to cause fundamental changes in world affairs which will also affect your labours in the gospel. *These changes will affect every area of life. They will affect the political atmosphere of the entire world, the economic and social atmosphere, and every level of human relations and of survival.*
>
> The system of the world as you know it is falling apart. The time is coming when every foundation that people are used to will give way to something new. The coming system will tighten its grip on the peoples of all nations. People will increasingly be driven by the events around them and these will drive them further and further away from the place of Grace. If you are going to see a major breakthrough in the nations, then you need to understand the connection between the *world system in the land and the way the people of that land respond to the gospel.* You also need to understand how important it is for you to disentangle yourself from the grip of the world around you. You are in the world but not of the world.'

At the time I did not realise how much this word related to September 11th and the changes that would follow it. I also did not realise what a major shift in the heavenlies it would create. However, I will come back to this point after I have elaborated on a few of the basic facts the word contained.

It slowly dawned upon me that people are products of their society and will live according to the dictates and expectations of their society. They will be constrained and limited by the world system in that society. This also means that as the world system changes within that society, the people living within it will also change their attitude toward life, and this also goes for their attitude toward God and the gospel. Consequently, even when those people have a hunger for God, they will be continually hindered and limited in their quest and experience of God according to the dictates of their society, unless these can be broken and they are set free.

This is already evident in Europe where the system and world view have changed immensely since the two world wars, from being fundamentally Christian to the present so-called 'Post-Christian Europe'. Consider how this has affected the corporate attitude of Europe's people toward God and the gospel in these nations. It affects not only the non-believers but also the believers in their depth of faith and experience of God.

It is especially sad when you consider the young generation, born into a society whose values have drifted so far away from God. They find themselves in a society in which the boundary between right and wrong has all but been removed and in which values are totally confused so that good is called evil, and evil good. Consider how this affects their openness to the gospel. Poor victims of history! I came to understand that people will only follow God to the degree that room for *spiritual freedom has been won within their world system. God is looking for men and women who will create this spiritual space for His people.* In the Great Commission the Church of Jesus Christ is called to be in the world but not of the world. Only then can it redeem God's people from the power of the world and its vices.

It was impressed upon me that the reason why the Church today is so lacking in impact as compared to the early Church is the degree to which God's people have allowed themselves to fall into the ranks of the world. This has caused us to lose whatever little influence we had and has weakened our ability to disciple nations. It also widens the gap between the Church and the people the Church is trying to win to Christ.

The Lord showed me prophetically that night that there will come a time (and very soon) when the Church, as it is today, will not be able to make any impact on these people, whatever it tries. Its message will be considered irrelevant by the very people it is trying to reach. Even some who are part of the Church as it is today will turn away and abandon it, believing that it provides no answers to the pressing issues of their lives. The kind of methods employed by the Church today (the church system, strategies, and approach of ministry) within the present world system will totally lose its impact. These methods will no longer be applicable or indeed relevant. The world will simply ignore the Church, regarding it as an irrelevant institution. *And this day is not far away.* If we are going to make any impact at such a time as this, we will need a total change of attitude and approach.

So What Should We Do?

I cried out in my heart to the Lord, 'Oh God, what must we do? How can we prepare for what is coming and overcome it?' The response was quick and direct:

> 'Set yourself apart for Me. Allow Me to work deeply in your life to release you from the hooks the world has in you. I will help you to overcome things you cannot overcome by yourself. I will cause your life to be separated from everything that hinders you from excelling in Me. I will lift you above the influences of your world and set you free from its bonds and limitations. I will give you authority over nations and peoples. I will cause people to be drawn to My light in your life in a way you could never have imagined possible. I will cause My Word through you to be much more effective than ever before. I will equip your life to accomplish things far beyond your own imagination, things otherwise impossible to you today.

All I am seeking is *a vessel set apart for Me*, totally separated
from the allurements and dictates of the world around,
and fully yielded to My will. If you want to know, this was
the secret of the early Church. It was the secret of everyone I ever used in generations gone by. It is still the secret
to My power today. As many people as will yield their
lives wholly to Me in this manner, I the Lord will always
honour' (John 12:24–26).

When I heard those words 'Set yourself apart for Me', I felt a
pang go through my heart, yet I did not grasp their full
meaning immediately. I thought that the Lord was calling
me into a time of fasting and prayer. I thought He was asking
me to lay down my plans for a while, and separate myself to
seek His face in seclusion for a period of time. So I cried out
immediately, 'Lord, I will do it. I will start whenever You tell
me. How many days should I fast? Lord, I am willing to fast as
long as You want me to. I am willing to go any distance to
gain this breakthrough.' I received no answer to this. There
was just an unnaturally pregnant silence in the Spirit which
left me with no doubt that I had missed something. Although
I prayed some more, the Spirit of the Lord did not say
anything else that night. As I was feeling exhausted I decided
to go to bed. I determined that I would wake up early and start
from where I had stopped. Before dawn, I woke up and again
resumed my prayer to the Lord. 'Father, give us the nations.
Show us what will break the prison gates to set Your people
free.'

Again the word of the Lord came to me, throwing more
light on the earlier words:

'The world is changing faster than you are adjusting, and
the issues you are dealing with are getting more and more
challenging. As a result you are getting caught up in the
sway of the world. So many of My servants have already
gone down this path and their work is increasingly losing
impact. I have spoken to them calling them apart to Me,

but they are so busy with the things the world has thrust before them that they keep putting Me off. They hear My call in their hearts but they are so engrossed with what they are doing that they have no time to heed My call. Some of what they are doing is My work but it is losing power because it is no longer coping with the trends in the world. Some of them are so busy trying to serve My people that they do not realise they are drifting further and further away from Me. My heart is grieving because I am losing them to the power of the world.

Unless you set yourself apart for Me, and allow Me to work deeply within you, you will also drift along on the same current. You will not even be able to stand in the days ahead. The enemy is raising his stakes. There are things that appeared harmless to you in the past that are now going to act like deadly hooks holding you back and not letting go. You will struggle hard to do what you know is right, but the hindrances in your life will be so strong that you will just fall short of the mark. Pay heed and hear My call: Set yourself apart for Me! This is My call to you. It is My call to all My people. Go out and say it out loud to all My people: whether they will hear or not. Go and be a witness to them. Tell them that this is My call of the hour! Set yourselves apart for Me and allow Me to prepare you for the times coming. Only those set apart for Me will be able to overcome in the times ahead.'

Again no directions were given concerning the period of fasting and seclusion which I thought I was being asked to undertake, but I did not feel anxious. I believed that clarity would come in due course.

World Trade Center Tragedy

When the time came for me to leave for my recording, I went down to the hotel lobby to meet the lady who had come to pick me up. She was the wife of the man who was then administrator of George Otis Jr's Sentinel Group. The first words she spoke to me were, 'John, isn't it terrible what has happened?' Perplexed, I asked what she meant. Expressing surprise that I was not aware of what had happened in New York that morning, she told me that a passenger plane had crashed into one of the twin towers of the World Trade Center in New York! At the time she was not aware of the full extent of the devastation. She led me to the television set in the hotel lobby so I could see the bizarre spectacle for myself. Strangely enough, my first thoughts were, 'God, Almighty, how many of the people in that tower were spiritually ready to meet their death?'

Then we drove to the venue where I was to do the recording. When we got there, we were told that it was not just one tower of the World Trade Center that had been hit, but both towers. Each tower had been hit by a separate plane. It became clear to all of us that this was no accident. It was a terrorist attack. Soon we also learnt that another plane had hit the Pentagon and yet another had crashed in Pennsylvania. There was confusion everywhere. The atmosphere was tense. George Otis Jr sent a message that in the circumstances he could not come to do his recording. It was suggested that I go ahead and do mine, which I did. But in the conditions that prevailed I don't think I made much sense. My mind was on other things.

As soon as I could, I got back to my hotel and began to follow the news on TV. Seeing those pictures and the shock of the nation of America, I could not help but be swallowed up by grief. I have seen suffering before in Uganda, not for just one day, but for years. Yes, I grew up under much suffering, but never before had I witnessed such heartbreak and emptiness as I experienced that week in the United States. One could feel the angry shock of a nation whose sense of security had been irreversibly shaken. The feeling of a safe haven had been violated, leaving a sense of panic in the air.

I felt personally affected. The pain in my heart was acute and was growing more and more intense as I watched the details unfold. In fact, I was so traumatised by the whole thing that for three weeks after I left the United States I could not sleep through the night. I would fall asleep for one or two hours and then remain awake for the rest of the night: the pictures of the terrorist attacks would stream through my mind, as well as thoughts of the bereaved who were mourning their loved ones in shock and agony. I began to take sleeping pills, but was advised to stop as it could easily lead to addiction.

Chapter 2

Sowing for Victory

On the night of the attack on the World Trade Center, as I watched TV, thoughts began to take shape in my mind which brought some understanding of the Lord's call for me to be set apart unto Him. Watching the repeated images of 'Ground Zero', the site of the former World Trade Center in New York, my attention was arrested by the New York Fire Department rescue workers. These men, who were frantically digging into the mountains of rubble in the hope of finding survivors, were the picture of gallantry itself. They were working under very dangerous conditions. Many of their colleagues had already lost their lives in the effort – and they too were at risk of being buried alive by the rubble at any moment. I marvelled at the courage and determination of these firefighters. The TV showed one who had worked straight through for many long hours without a break. When asked if he did not think he needed to take a rest, he replied, 'Someone in there may be hanging on, depending on us to get to them in the next few minutes. How can I rest knowing that to be true?'

I heard of another man, also a rescue worker, who had run up into one of the towers to help people escape before it collapsed. Someone shouted to him to abandon the rescue effort and get out because it was too dangerous. The rescue worker replied that he couldn't leave as long as there were people in there whose lives he could save. It was reported that he called his wife on the phone, telling her that he didn't know whether he was going to make it out of the building. He wanted her to know that he had always loved her and enjoyed being married to her. *He never came out alive!*

Hundreds of other rescue workers perished as they tried to save lives. Many of them died gallantly, knowingly risking their own safety for the sake of others. I marvelled at the commitment, courage, determination and selflessness of these men. They could have spared their own lives if they had chosen to, but they chose not to. As I watched, the Spirit of the Lord said to me,

> 'What those men are doing today is not a result of a decision that they made this morning. It is not a decision they made as a reaction to the tragedy you are watching now. Many years ago, each of them made a decision to join a profession that would demand selfless service to save others' lives.'

That decision shaped their destiny. They underwent training and preparation for crises of all sorts. They allowed themselves to be trained (*call it programmed*) to cope with extreme conditions of tension and danger. In their training, any personal weaknesses that would easily compromise them were identified and dealt with. The discipline that would make them strong enough and bold enough to deal with any circumstance they might face was steadily incorporated into their inner fabric. None of this was achieved in a matter of days. It took time slowly to change their priorities and values. They learned to despise the things that matter so much to other people, the things that would hold them back. They learned to uphold values that most people dismiss as too high. In other words, a long time ago they *set themselves apart* for such a task and time as this. When the day came, they were there and they were ready!

If placed in similar circumstances, many well-meaning people would just turn and run for their lives without feeling any sense of guilt, and that is precisely what happened in New York. It was the most sensible thing for any sane person to do.

To run for their life! Yet the attitude of these firefighters was different. To them the logical thing was not to run away, but to plunge themselves into the danger and save a life while the opportunity existed. The only reason they were able to do this was because long ago they invested time and effort in preparing their lives to function above circumstances such as these. As I pondered these words, the Spirit of the Lord very softly said to me,

> 'The call to be set apart is *not about going away for a few days of fasting and prayer*. It is a call to a long-term sowing into a new lifestyle. It is a call out of one lifestyle, which looks so logical and right to other people, into another lifestyle programmed for victory and the ability to stand where others would fall or turn and run. What the nations need today is a new breed of God's people that live their lives above the constraints that hold others back. People who have learnt to despise the things that trap and hold back everyone else. People who have allowed themselves to have a dynamic encounter with God through which the Lord Himself makes them vessels of honour. If you will allow yourself to start on this journey, I will work deeply in your life to do for you what you cannot do for yourself. I will change your attitude toward life. I will separate you from things that weaken your heart. And I will make you able to stand where many would just fall or give in to pressure. You will be an overcomer; then I will position you to help My people worldwide in the times ahead.'

It was not an audible voice but it was very powerful. Sometimes God speaks in ways that words cannot describe.

There was now a new piece to the puzzle. If being set apart is not about *a few days of fasting*, then what indeed was it about,

and how did one go about it? Another illustration soon came
my way. As I continued to watch the news updates on TV, I
was deeply disturbed by the repeated pictures of the terrorist
planes being flown straight into the World Trade Center
towers. I asked myself, 'What were those pilots thinking
during those last moments? They were aware that all the
passengers on board, as well as the people inside the World
Trade Center, were innocent unsuspecting individuals with
loved ones waiting to see them back home. What went
through the minds of the pilots in those final moments as
they approached the towers, watching those towers draw
closer and closer, and knowing that they themselves were
going to die along with everyone else? How could anybody be
so heartless? How did their hearts become so hardened that
they did not flinch in the slightest from what they were about
to do?' I wondered whether they felt fear or just crazy elation!
    Then my thoughts changed direction. These men were
professionals! They had invested a great deal of time and
money in their education and flight training! They had bright
prospects and could have made good money and have
prospered! So what on earth would cause such individuals to
give it all up, and choose to fly jet planes into high-rise
buildings to sure, inescapable death? Suddenly my mind
cleared, and the answers seemed to unfold. Those men were
not acting on impulse. They did not wake up that morning
and decide that it might be a good idea to undertake a suicide
mission. It was not something that they did because they saw
an opportunity. Many years before, these men must have
made a choice. There was a moment in the life of each of them
when they decided to lay down their lives for a cause they
believed in. It does not matter that you and I don't believe in
their cause: what is important is to note the principle that
paved the way for such a mission.
    When these men joined the ranks of their fanatical organi-
sations, they knew what they were signing up for. They went
and trained. They learned to overcome fear, feelings and
anything else that would hamper their suicidal mission. They

distanced themselves from the things that mean everything to the rest of us, the things that are important to us as 'normal people'. They learned to despise and deny the values that would cause any of the rest of us to pause and reconsider. Their priorities in life were grossly altered, and they lived a life that was already given over to death. Their cause was all that mattered to them. Some of them even had families, but they kept their mission secret from their wives and children. They gave up a life that other men labour for. When the moment came for their hideous mission, they did not pull back. They had no thoughts of retreat even as they approached their sure death. They destroyed thousands of lives without flinching.

What made all this possible was the *initial long-term investment they had made in becoming the people they were*. There was a moment in their lives when they separated themselves from the influences of their worlds, and laid down their lives for a cause they were willing to live and die for. They overcame all human weaknesses that would have held them back, through the discipline of a life sown into a cause.

Now it all made sense to me. I could now understand the call of God to be set apart unto Him. A few days alone in fasting and prayer was not *necessarily* what God was calling me to. This was a much longer and deeper undertaking. It was a call to sow my life into the cause I believed in: the Great Commission! This was the cause of transforming nations and cities with the power of God: opening up the spiritual atmosphere and bringing God's kingdom into communities; gathering in the harvest of my Lord who laid down His life for me and the lost multitudes out there.

Once again I realised why the Church, as it is today, is actually weak and entangled in the ways and values of the world. Most of us react to situations in exactly the same way the world does. Many of the things that are so dear to us, while *good* in themselves end up hindering our very obedience to God. Where we should be expecting to lay down our lives for our faith, we flinch from it because it is simply inconceivable to us. We want to transform our communities for Jesus, but we are part of the very fabric of sickness we want to do away with. If we are going to make a real difference, we are going to have to rise above the impediments of our communities and cultures. We are going to have to shed a lot of things we cherish. Our priorities will have to change and so will our discipline. But in exchange, we stand to get into a place of confidence with God that opens up a whole new range of godly exploits. This is what the giants of faith in the book of Hebrews chapter 11 experienced.

That evening as I was praying, the Lord said,

> 'This call of separation unto Me is not just to you alone. *This is the call of the hour for my people worldwide.* Separate yourselves unto Me and I will separate you from your weaknesses. I will make you the people I will use to overturn nations and cities in these last days. I will gather in your loved ones, transform your communities and bring glory to My name. I want you to tell this to My people everywhere you go.'

By calling us to be set apart for Him, the Lord is seeking to take us to levels far beyond what we would be capable of in normal circumstances. We need to go that extra mile if we are to make any meaningful impact on the nations of our generation. Some of these things we truly cannot do for ourselves, we don't even know how. Some weaknesses and shortcomings we are not even aware of but in the process of being *set apart*, the Lord will do exceedingly, abundantly above what we can ask or even imagine.

Chapter 3

Set Apart: Bible Examples

Having been stopped in my tracks by this call, I became more and more gripped by it. While I remained deeply concerned about New York and the terrorist attacks, I was desperate for a deeper understanding of what was unfolding in my spirit. I turned to the Scriptures to see if I could find any reference to the concept of being set apart, and I was not disappointed. Over the next few days, I discovered that the call to be set apart appears to be *God's precondition* to major interventions in human affairs. I saw that every time God wanted to bring about a fundamental change in His dealings with human beings, He called out a people or an individual and set them apart for Himself. He called them out of the system they were used to, out of their constraints, their environment and comfort zones. Then He worked in their lives in such a way that they were totally transformed and were able to accomplish things that were previously impossible for them.

Abraham

The story of Abraham was the first to come to mind. Humankind was lost, and God wanted to begin the process of redemption. His plan was to establish one race which He would use to demonstrate His nature and character in such a way that the lost world would eventually choose to return to Him. But how could He ensure that the people He would take as His own would not become like the rest of humankind?

After all they would live in the midst of the others! How could He keep His chosen people from adopting the mindset and world view of the rest of the human race?

It is how people think and view life that causes them to live the way they do.

God chose to ensure this separation by calling one man out from the rest and setting him apart for His purpose, and then making an infallible covenant with him. That way the anchor of the deal was God Himself and not man. That man would be able to live above the bondages and constraints of his generation. Thus, Abraham was called out of his culture, traditions, attitudes and the lifestyle of his generation. He was called out so that he could embrace wholeheartedly the full revelation of God's counsel and enable the Lord to fulfil His plan and promises in him. In Genesis 12:1–3 we read:

> 'Now the LORD had said to Abram:
>   "Get out of your country,
>   From your family
>   And from your father's house,
>   To a land that I will show you.
>   I will make you a great nation;
>   I will bless you
>   And make your name great;
>   And you shall be a blessing.
>   I will bless those who bless you,
>   And I will curse him who curses you;
>   And in you all the families of the earth shall be blessed." '

The people of Abraham's time were descendants of Noah, saved from the flood and survivors by grace, but all of them had sunk into grave depravity that ended up in the confusion of Babel and consequently the great dispersion (Genesis 11:1–9). So God called Abraham out from his family, from his country, his environment, his cultural constraints and all other types of limitations. God promised to make out of him a new nation, which would be called by God's own name. God told Abraham that through this new nation He would bless all humankind. In other words this would be a special nation, a nation set apart for the very purpose of God redeeming the lost nations of the world. God needed a new foundation. He needed a people with different values, a different world view. Through Abraham's obedience in being set apart for God, a channel was made available through which God could reach out to all humankind with the way of salvation.

Total Depravity

When we look at human history, it seems that eventually human beings sink to such a level of depravity and their minds become so corrupted that they literally go beyond the point of *logical reform*. Even if they know God's truth they can only sink into further depravity (see Romans 1:28–32). When human beings reach this point, there is no longer anything to revive in them. No preaching or prophesying can get through to them! Even prayer can only achieve very little. It is as if God would say, 'Don't ask Me to bless them, for there is no way I can do it. Don't ask Me to help them for I will not.' (See Isaiah 59:1–2 and Jeremiah 7:16–19.)

Yes! Some things will change easily through prayer, but there are others that are so rotten that even when we pray, *God will not pour new wine into old wineskins, or patch new cloth onto old garments* (see Luke 5:36–39). But even in such circumstances God does not give up on His people. Instead He demands new beginnings. He seeks a people who will disentangle themselves from the system of their day and consecrate themselves to Him. When He finds them He prepares them to be *vehicles of change*. Through them He initiates transformation of whole communities and nations that otherwise would have been doomed (see Judges 13:1–5).

This was the state of things in Abraham's days. There was some sort of knowledge of God among the peoples, but it was so clouded that they instead worshipped all kinds of things and called them their gods. Even people in Abraham's own home made no distinction between the true God and false gods. Let us now look at another example of a life set apart for God that was used to break through an impossible system.

Samuel

The state of depravity existing in many nations today actually means that the same radical step as Abraham took is required from Christians, even in nations traditionally known as Christian. Moral decay has eaten so deeply into communities that it has come to be accepted as normal.

Even when intercessors make prayer for revival or transformation in the nations, so much remains clouded in the *mindset of the day* that God finds it hard to align our prayers with His heart. *Maybe this is why so much prayer seems to go unanswered today.*

In 1 Samuel 3:1 we read:

> *'Now the boy Samuel ministered to the LORD before Eli. And the word of the LORD was rare in those days; there was no widespread revelation.'*

We must note that no prayer could change Israel because there was no word from God. Prayer without utterance from the throne-room is ineffective prayer. Prayer is effective only as it yokes with the word that comes from the Lord, because no word that comes from the Lord will ever be devoid of power. When there is no word coming directly from God, no prayer can revive the land. At such a time, God will look for a man or woman who will stand in the gap and be set apart. Samuel was such a man. God had to come to him, bypassing all the 'seasoned' ministers and even the high priest.

Samuel was born at a time when things were very bad in Israel. Eli was the high priest in the temple of the Lord and his sons were priests with him, but the spiritual state of the land was rotten. The Bible says that the word of God was scarce and there was no revelation: no vision! That simply means that most of the preaching at that time was just human wisdom and most probably manipulation of people's minds. After all, the priests went on preaching even if God no longer spoke to them. In 1 Samuel 2:12 the conclusion is reached:

'Now the sons of Eli were corrupt; they did not know the Lord.'

It is even on record that the priests were wicked and did not know the Lord. As a result there was no vision in Israel. No one knew what God was doing or wanted to do. NO VISION!

Things had become so bad that in 1 Samuel 2:13–15 we are told:

'And the priests' custom with the people was that when any man offered a sacrifice, the priest's servant would come with a three-pronged fleshhook in his hand while the meat was boiling. Then he would thrust it into the pan, or kettle, or cauldron, or pot; and the priest would take for himself all that the fleshhook brought up. So they did in Shiloh to all the Israelites who came there. Also, before they burned the fat, the priest's servant would come and say to the man who sacrificed, "Give meat for roasting to the priest, for he will not take boiled meat from you, but raw."'

Sin was the order of the day not only among the people but also among the very priests who ministered to God in the temple. Greed was their driving force! They were out to get whatever they could from the people without any fear of the name of the Lord. In this way they abused the offering of the Lord and the sacrifice of His people:

'Therefore the sin of the young men was very great before the Lord, for men abhorred the offering of the Lord.' (verse 17)

It was so bad that the people even became weary of giving or sacrificing to the Lord. In the New American Standard Bible it says that people came to 'despise' the offering of the Lord. They abhorred and detested it.

Not only were the priests greedy and manipulative about God's offering but they sunk into deeper and deeper sins until they were committing fornication with the women who assembled in the temple, and all Israel knew about it (1 Samuel 2:22).

Just imagine the following scenario: an Israelite man has had some misfortunes in his life and family, and wants to come and give offerings to God at Shiloh. He feels his offerings will bring some general good fortune to his life. Therefore he prepares his unblemished first-born lamb and takes it to Shiloh. When he arrives there, it is taken by the Levites and, as Moses instructed, he lays hands on its head, makes his prayer requests and the lamb is taken away to be slaughtered and offered.

When the slaughter has been carried out and the animal is put on the fire for sacrifice, right before his very eyes, a servant comes from Phinehas and Hophni and demands the meat that is still on the altar, but the Levite refuses to give it to him and a scuffle ensues. The servant pushes him away, grabs a fork, plunges it into whatever piece he can and takes away the sizzling meat to Phinehas and his brother. What is this poor Israelite to think? He has banked all his hope on a sacrifice that would please God and yet it has been desecrated before his eyes. He has no power to rebuke these 'men of God'. He cannot get back at them. He is angry, bitter, wounded, unfulfilled, and sees no hope in God. So he goes back home, and all his rage against the 'untouchable men of God' is released on those weaker than him: his wife, children and servants.

The wife becomes unhappy with the situation at home and does not understand her husband's strange behaviour. She cannot turn to him for solace or answers, so she resolves to turn to God. Maybe God will hear her many anxieties concerning the object of her misery, her husband. Maybe if she goes to Shiloh she can seek counsel from the priests. She makes her journey to Shiloh to give her offerings, worship God and present her petitions. She gets there and is exposed to the same desecration of her offering and, even worse, she is disrespected and defiled by the 'men of God'. She too gets back home bitter, hurt, abused, angry at the 'men of God' and at her husband; she turns on those weaker than her to release her bitterness – the children and any servants in the home.

The children know that their parents are religious, yet they cannot understand the paradox of their inconsistent behaviour. They watch their parents go to give sacrifice and worship at Shiloh and come home with bad attitudes and words. When they go to Shiloh with their parents, they see how they pretend to be righteous and happy before the men of God, and draw the conclusion that they themselves can act righteous and go through the motions before their parents and other people but carry on in a sinful riotous life amongst their peers, where those in authority over them cannot see them. Unable to relate to the adults' double-standards they revile authorities and have no respect for God. It was this kind of scenario that created the system of life in Israel at that time.

When God's people are brought to this point, not just among themselves but also among the priests of God, they begin to lose hope in God. They also lose hope in prayer. They lose hope in sacrificing to God. It all ceases to be meaningful. When people lose hope in God they become self-dependent and headstrong. They also become selfish and self-indulgent. The practice of religion or faith becomes a mere ritual they go through just for the sake of it: 'going through the motions'.

If God's servants do this to the people, what kind of priesthood would you expect men to show in their own families? Would they have the foundation they need in order to be examples in their own homes? Would they manage to build the faith of their children in God and to raise them up in the fear of God?

If men feel abused by the very priests who represent God to them, would they not in turn find themselves abusing their wives and children in their own homes? Would they also not pursue their own selfish desires in the name of God? Or would it not be easier for them just to forget about God once they leave the temple and are back in their homes?

If children witnessed this behaviour of both the priests in the temple and their own parents at home, would they not conclude that the whole idea of God and purity was nothing but a mere joke that no one took seriously? Would they have the will to resist peer pressure when it pushed them to dishonour God?

Oh! The list of implications just goes on and on and on. Such a vicious cycle of depravity is very difficult to break. We read in 1 Samuel 2:22–25 that Eli heard about what his children were doing to all Israel. He knew also that not only did they sin, but they made 'God's people transgress'. It was no secret. He talked to them. He preached to them and made it clear that what they were doing was not good, was not holy, and was neither befitting of their office nor acceptable to God. BUT...! They did not change. There comes a time when people have sunk so low that even the preaching of what is right and wrong does not change them anymore. They know that those who do such things deserve to die but they not only do these very same things themselves, they also approve of others who practise them (Romans 1:32).

Then God sent a prophet to speak to Eli, the high priest, about the state of the nation Israel (1 Samuel 2:27–36). The prophet's message contained both rebuke and judgement:

- God rebuked Eli for allowing his sons to profane the offering of the Lord, and use it instead to fatten themselves.
- God rebuked Eli for honouring his sons more than Him.
- God told Eli that He honours those who honour Him and those who despise Him He brings to nought.
- God pronounced judgement upon Eli, his sons and his entire line of descendants, if they did not repent.
- God gave him specific signs that would confirm His judgement when it came.
- God even said that though He would do good to His people Israel, Eli and his household would still suffer the judgements promised. This sounds like a desperate attempt to make Eli finally wake up to his plight.

One would have expected immediate repentance from Eli and his sons, but this did not happen. Maybe they were saddened when they heard the prophet's warning but their hearts had become far too hard. I am sure that deep within they wanted to repent; who would not? But it did not happen.

One can reach a place where one's heart has grown cold. When that place has been reached, even a very clear word of prophecy will cause that person only to acknowledge that 'indeed God has spoken', but he or she will not repent. People reach a place where they just have *no strength left* in them to repent. When they hear the word they agree with it, but for some reason they postpone the idea of acting on it. They will promise themselves that 'tomorrow or next week I will deal with these issues', but there is always something that diverts them. In the end they just continue in their sins, even though they actually hate themselves for what they are doing. Even if they are aware that God has warned them about impending judgement, they still cannot find the will to turn away from their sins and repent. Sometimes they even seek to find theological backing to give them some solace in the place of their depravity rather than repent and find life. This is a very dangerous place to be; yet unfortunately that is where multitudes of God's people are today.

In His love and mercy God does not rush to bring judgement upon us. Neither did He rush to judge Eli. He came into Eli's house one night and began to call the boy Samuel.

When Samuel eventually opened up to listen to God, God told him about the impending judgement on the house of Eli. There was urgency in the message. It seems as if it was a last-minute attempt by God to save Eli and his household from having to face judgement. But when Eli found out what God had said about him the next morning, did he repent?

No!

Was he shaken?

No!

He simply said, *'It is the LORD. Let Him do what seems good to Him.'*

Can you imagine that? The man was too far gone. Let me warn you, my dear readers, that when people cease to care about what happens, they have reached the point where they can only die and nothing else. There is no way of saving them. If you find that it no longer matters to you what happens, then you should be aware that death has got its clutches on your soul. In Eli's case, soon the inevitable happened. Judgement befell the house of Eli like a whirlwind. We are told what happened in 1 Samuel 4:1–22:

- In one day the Ark of the Lord, the most treasured object that God had entrusted into the keeping of the priests, was captured.
- The two priestly sons of Eli, Hophni and Phinehas, were killed at the battle front, where they had been in charge of the Ark of the Lord.
- Eli, on receiving the news about his sons and the Ark of the Lord, fell from his chair and broke his neck, dying immediately.
- When his daughter-in-law, heavy with child, heard of the death of her husband, Phinehas, and Eli her father-in-law, as well as the loss of the Ark of the Lord, she went into labour. She gave birth to a son but died as a result of the effort.
- As she died, the women around her tried to encourage her by informing her that she had given birth to a son, but *'she named the child Ichabod, saying, "The glory has departed from Israel!"'*

In just one day all the judgements of the Lord against Eli and his household were fulfilled. But that was not the end. Although later the Lord visited Israel with grace and mercy, the house of Eli continued under the yoke it had brought upon itself, just as had been prophesied. When I read all this, a chill goes down my spine. This is a terrible ending for a man who had such a great calling in God. And yet the same conditions that led to such a sad ending are so common in our day. There is such a degree of sin in the house of the Lord today, both among the people and among the priests or pastors of the Lord, that many things are no longer called sin anymore. They have been made acceptable – otherwise everybody would be called 'a sinner', *and that sounds pretty uncomfortable.*

Even when it becomes common knowledge that sin is going on in the house of the Lord, we permit things to continue as usual, just as Eli did in his day. We, in effect, honour each other above God. The same spirit of greed that was in Eli's sons has eaten away at the church directly from the pulpit. Immorality has gone so far that today perverted men practising open abominations are appointed as church leaders in direct contradiction of God's Word.

God's Word, which tells us that these things are wrong, is still sometimes preached, just as Eli attempted to say something to his sons about their lifestyle; but now as then, no one pays any heed and there is no change. Prophets come and speak clearly to us in our churches and in our conferences. Like Eli we acknowledge that God has spoken to us, but we lack the power to repent. We want to change but we feel unable to. Even when we experience God's presence so strongly that we are convinced of His claims about us, we simply shrug it off as Eli did. 'We are just mortal beings,' we say. 'He is sovereign; let Him do what seems right to Him.' Meanwhile we continue in our lifestyles and comfort ourselves by listening to teachers that make our ears tickle with things we enjoy hearing.

Beloved, in such conditions, prayer really will not avail much on its own. There is a need for someone to separate him- or herself from this trend and cry out persistently to God for a fresh intervention from above. In the days of Eli, this was Samuel. Samuel was a man set apart for God. Every time the Bible describes the depravity of the time, it mentions clearly that Samuel was different:

- *'But the child ministered to the LORD before Eli the priest'* (1 Samuel 2:11).

- *'But Samuel ministered before the* Lord, *even as a child . . . '* (1 Samuel 2:18).
- *'And the child Samuel grew in stature and in favour both with the* Lord *and men'* (1 Samuel 2:26).
- *' . . . the boy Samuel ministered to the* Lord *before Eli'* (1 Samuel 3:1).
- *'So Samuel grew, and the* Lord *was with him and let none of his words fall to the ground. And all Israel from Dan to Beersheba knew that Samuel had been established as a prophet of the* Lord. *Then the* Lord *appeared again in Shiloh. For the* Lord *revealed Himself to Samuel in Shiloh by the word of the* Lord*'* (1 Samuel 3:19–21).
- *'And the word of Samuel came to all Israel'* (1 Samuel 4:1).

We are left in no doubt that when God is faced with an impossible situation as He was in the days of Eli, it is only a life *set apart for Him* which will move Him to act on behalf of His people. And if our day is very similar to Eli's day, then it is easy to understand why today God is looking for individuals who will set themselves apart for Him so that He can transform them into vessels for change.

Unfortunately, there are many people today who have heard this call from God to set themselves apart for Him so that He might use them for great things, and who understand what God is calling them to, yet keep playing the procrastination game. They are full of excuses, based on reasoning that only breeds disobedience. Even as I write this I feel a shudder go through me. The Spirit of God is so grieved by this matter that I can literally feel His pain as I sit writing.

My plea to those who understand what I am talking about right now is, *please don't wait too long.* One day it will be too late. I don't think Eli knew how close it had come until it actually hit him. Don't let this be your plight.

Chapter 4

Idols of the Heart

I mentioned earlier that when the Lord first spoke to me about being set apart, I thought He wanted me to take time out for a fast. However, as He led me to look at the September 11th examples of the New York firefighters and of the terrorists, about which I spoke in Chapter 2, and as He revealed the entire concept of being set apart through the biblical examples I have just examined with you, I realised that it was not that easy.

The call is to a long journey, to a lifestyle of total consecration. I was willing to start out on this journey, but could not actually put my finger on how to begin. So I asked the Lord. I prayed for guidance and revelation. The answer came in words I least expected. 'Son, with all sincerity, would you say that you are *being* your best for Me in your life?'

I hope, dear reader, that you notice the strangeness of this question. He did not say, 'Are you *doing* your best for Me?', but 'Are you *being* . . .'.

I immediately understood that the Lord was focusing on *how I live my life for Him on a daily basis*, not on what I do in ministry for Him.

In a flash, into my mind sprang four different areas in which I knew clearly I was not *being* my best for God. These are areas I had talked to God about several times in the past. I had promised Him and myself many times that I would get my act together. Yet for some reason, I had kept postponing taking action. I knew deep in my heart that if I really determined to deal with them I had the ability to do so. It was perfectly possible. But for some reason I just kept putting that decision off. Now, however, the moment of truth had come and I had to be sincere with myself and with my God.

I immediately responded by beginning to repent and confess my failure, promising to start dealing with the issues right away. But the Lord cut me short. He said, 'Write down all those areas which you know you are holding back from Me.'

I felt my blood rush to my face and anger rising. 'Why should I write down four very distinct things I could name without having to see them on paper?' Nevertheless, I obeyed and wrote them down. As I did so, something else sprang to my mind which I added to my list as a fifth area. Then immediately another also came up, then another and yet another. My list grew quite rapidly until there were sixteen items on it. I was shocked! 'Oh my God, all these are areas I am holding back from You in one way or another!' I knew I was perfectly able to move all the way, and could have done so _any time I chose_ but somehow I had always held back.

'So why do you hold back?' the clear voice of the Holy Spirit asked me.

Yes, why? Why did I hold back from that which I knew was the best for me? Why did I hold back from that which I desired so much inwardly? I knew without a doubt that, given a chance, I would not choose any other way than the way of the Lord, yet as I lived my life in the free choice that the Lord allows me daily, this is not what I had done. I instead chose the opposite and kept promising myself that tomorrow I would change for the better.

Then again it dawned upon me that this indeed was the measure of the love of God I had in my heart. Although I always said that I loved the Lord with all my heart, I was being clearly shown that my love was half-hearted, divided and given grudgingly.

The Lord then led me to write down all the excuses I normally use to keep me from being what I know I could be in fullness for God. I felt so silly because all the excuses suddenly appeared hollow and empty. How could I ever have allowed such foolishness to blind me?

The Lord showed me that behind each excuse was the real reason why I could not be what I desired to be in Him. I was led to examine myself and find out why such silly and unconvincing excuses have always satisfied my heart into living with less, when I could have the whole counsel of God for me. As I slowly listed these, the Spirit said to me,

'Now you are touching the idols of your heart. These are the things that you love and regard more highly than you love and regard Me: the ones you honour above Me, in the same way that Eli honoured his sons above Me. When they demand your attention, it does not matter that you know My will; you will always find a way of obeying them instead of Me. This is what keeps you from being the man I want you to be for Me. Deep inside you also desire and crave the same, yet you will always stop before you get there unless *you overcome*. There are things you will never achieve in your life until you remove those idols from your heart. I, the Lord, hate idolatry.'

I was reminded of Ezekiel 14:1–4:

'Now some of the elders of Israel came to me and sat before me. And the word of the LORD came to me, saying, "Son of man, these men have set up their idols in their hearts, and put before them that which causes them to stumble into iniquity. Should I let Myself be inquired of at all by them? Therefore speak to them, and say to them, 'Thus says the Lord GOD: "Everyone of the house of Israel who sets up his idols in his heart, and puts before him what causes him to stumble into iniquity, and then comes to the prophet, I the LORD will answer him who comes, according to the multitude of his idols ... " ' " ' '

Vision

I saw a vision before my eyes of a man who had hooks sticking out of his back. The enemy was able to throw ropes into these hooks. The ropes were long and allowed the man a lot of freedom, so he appeared to be able to do a lot for God.

However, whenever he was inspired to go all the way for God, he would move forward but he could only go as far as the ropes would allow. When they were fully stretched, he would be restrained. No matter how much he tried, he could not go further than the ropes hooked to his back permitted.

The Lord showed me that this is what happens to us when we entertain idols in our lives. The idols act as hooks in our backs. The enemy just has to throw his ropes into them and we are restrained. We may seem to be able to do a lot of things, but any time we try to go beyond what the *system* around us permits, we are immediately restrained. We end up doing much in our own eyes, but only producing results possible within human limitations.

Many have accepted this as the fullness of their ministry. The Great Commission is about discipling whole nations for Christ but most ministries have given up this dream for a much smaller one of only looking at how much they can achieve as single ministries. However, with the challenges posed by this changing world, God knows the futility of such ministry. This is why He calls us be set apart unto Him. If we allow Him, He will work deeply in our lives to separate us from the things that we cannot separate ourselves from.

There are some things holding us back which are so deep in us that even we don't recognise them for what they are: hooks of darkness! We never confess them. We have never even thought of dealing with them. But if we are set apart to God, He will reveal them, deal with them and separate us from them. This will in turn make us into vessels of honour in the hand of the Master.

Beloved, anything that competes with God for the love and control of our hearts is *an idol*. It does not always have to be some big ugly thing. Most of the time, those idols are 'innocent excuses', 'valid reasons', or 'harmless amusements'. But they have one thing in common: they will always provide us with a 'good excuse' for failing to live up to the requirements of God.

*'Therefore, to him who knows to do good and does not do it, to
him it is sin.'*   (James 4:17)

God is grieved and saddened by the idols we put before Him in
our hearts. And He says these idols cause us to stumble and
fall. They limit us. We may want to go all the way with God
but the idols in our hearts cause us to fail. However innocent
they may appear, they are responsible for our failing to excel
in God and for falling short of what we ourselves would love
to be for Him.

This is not to say that our performance before God is purely
dependent on our ability alone. I want to contrast the lives of
two men in the Bible to show how God's grace is demon-
strated to a man who is set apart to Him as opposed to one
who is not.

David and Saul

David and Saul are men whose beginnings and experiences are
so similar in many ways and yet their ends could not be more
different. Both of them came from families of little worldly
significance until the two men were exalted by God. Both
of them were keepers of animals. Both were sought out and
found by the same man, Samuel. Both were anointed by the
same prophet to become kings. Both became not only kings
but also prophets.

During their reign both of them sinned against God. Both
of them are on record as having confessed their sin, or
somehow sought restoration.

BUT . . . !

God forgave one and rejected the other. One, David, was
able to find restoration and finally died in the Lord, while his
counterpart, Saul, deteriorated so much that he became a
demoniac craving after innocent life. He died having fallen so
far away that he had to seek the counsel of witches to find out
the will of God.

What was the great difference between these two generals of God?

David came from a background of being set apart for God right from the beginning. Even before he was anointed for kingship, Samuel reported, *'The LORD has sought for Himself a man after His own heart'* (1 Samuel 13:14). He is one of the men of God we see in the Scriptures who was indeed set apart for God. He had his heart set on God.

Saul was also a man who loved the Lord and fought many a battle in God's name. He did many wonderful things for Israel. However, unlike David, Saul's heart was set on pleasing the people and maintaining a good image before them. The fact that it was God who had actually made him king didn't matter very much to him. For the people's sake he readily went against God's wishes.

The first instance is in 1 Samuel 13:1–14 which tells how Saul prepared for war in the understanding that Samuel would join him on the seventh day and offer a sacrifice to God before the army went out to fight. However, before Samuel arrived, the Philistine army gathered and set up camp in sight of the Jews. When they saw the large numbers of Philistines, the men of Israel lost heart and started to hide in caves, thickets, rocks and pits. Some even crossed the Jordan to the lands of Gad and Gilead.

When Saul saw that his men were deserting him, everything within him went into panic and he decided that rather than wait for Samuel any longer, he would go ahead and perform the priestly duty of offering the sacrifice, even though that was not his office.

Just after he had done so, Samuel appeared and inquired what the King had done. Saul's answer is very telling, *'When I saw that the people were scattered from me ...'* Judgement was prompt and immediate: the kingship would not be passed on to his descendants.

Later the Lord sent him on a mission to attack and totally destroy the Amalekites because of the evil they had committed against the people of Israel (1 Samuel 15:2–3). He was not to leave a single one of them alive. But Saul did not do exactly as the Lord had commanded. The Bible tells us that

Saul and the people were *'unwilling'* to utterly destroy every-thing as the Lord had commanded (1 Samuel 15:9). They were just unwilling!

On returning from battle, Saul felt so good at having carried out a successful mission for God, that he even went to Carmel and erected a monument to himself as a memorial. But while he was celebrating the Lord's victory through him, God in heaven was grieving over him for rejecting His word and instead choosing to do his own bidding (1 Samuel 15:10–12).

Beloved, this scenario is being repeated daily in our churches today. Many of God's servants could not care less about whether they are carrying out God's instructions to them in full obedience or not. They do their own thing in the name of the Lord while congratulating themselves for having obeyed God. People may look at our lives outwardly and say, 'Oh, great man (or woman) of God, obedient to God and wholly following Him', but on the inside we know that we are living in disobedience. We should not allow the applause of people to deceive us into celebrating what we know is our disobedience as if it were obedience.

People only see what is on the surface, but we know what is going on on the inside. We can tell when we are not pleasing God. Heaven may be grieving over our lives, while on earth we are celebrated as wonderful, obedient giants of God. 'That pastor is a mighty man of God,' the people say. 'See how his church is so full of life and fire!' In heaven, God is saying, 'I regret that I ever sent this man to start that congregation. He is living in disobedience. He is not doing what I sent him to do. He is running the work according to his own plans. All he cares about is what people think of him and not My purpose for the work I have placed in his hands.'

That was exactly the case with King Saul. When he met Samuel, he proudly reported that he had done what the Lord had sent him to do: destroyed the Amalekites and their belongings, including their animals. Samuel then asked about the bleating of sheep and lowing of cattle he was hearing in his prophet's ears. Saul answered, 'Oh they are from the

Amalekites. You know *the people* spared the best sheep and oxen *to sacrifice to the* LORD *your God; and the rest we have utterly destroyed'* (v. 15). Surely Samuel should be happy, after all the people were so thoughtful? *But were they?*

Notice how Saul brought in 'the people'. God's instructions to him were very clear. He had chosen not to do as God had required, but here he was, saying it was the people who had acted contrary to God's word. When Samuel put it to him that he had not obeyed the Lord, Saul was unrepentant. Why had he taken the spoil and spared Agag the Amalekite king? Saul argued that he had fully obeyed the Lord. He had gone on the mission on which God had sent him. The only slight difference was that the people had insisted on taking back the best of the sheep and oxen. He would not take the blame. He saw the whole thing as really 'no big deal'. 'Come on, Samuel, it is not really that bad! We only saved the best to sacrifice to your God. Come on, look at it from our perspective. See the people's point of view. After all, generally speaking, we really did obey God, didn't we? We destroyed the Amalekites!'

There is much service of this kind to our God today. I pray that all of us would examine ourselves lest we finish in the same way as Saul.

A careful examination of Saul's life will show us that he had a problem which Samuel actually called *idolatry*. In 1 Samuel 13:11 in the case of the offering he should not have made, he explained his action by saying: *'When I saw* **that the people were scattered from me** ... ' (my emphasis). In 1 Samuel 15:15 when Samuel confronted Saul about the Amalekite mission, the King replied, *'**the people spared** the best of the sheep and the oxen, to sacrifice to the* LORD *your God; and the rest we have utterly destroyed'* (my emphasis). When Samuel accused him of disobedience to the Lord, Saul answered,

> *'But I have obeyed the voice of the* LORD *and gone on the mission on which the* LORD *sent me ... but the people took of the plunder ... to sacrifice to the* LORD *... '*
>
> (1 Samuel 15:20–21)

Samuel answered Saul,

> *'Has the* LORD *as great delight in burnt offerings and*
>   *sacrifices,*
> *As in obeying the voice of the* LORD*?*
> *Behold, to obey is better than sacrifice,*
> *And to heed than the fat of rams.*
> *For rebellion is as the sin of witchcraft,*
> *And stubbornness is as iniquity and idolatry.*
> *Because you have rejected the word of the* LORD*,*
> *He also has rejected you from being king.'*
>
> (1 Samuel 15:22–23)

Saul replied,

> *'I have sinned, for I have transgressed the commandment of*
> *the* LORD *and your words,* **because I feared the people and**
> **obeyed their voice** *...'*   (1 Samuel 15:24, my emphasis)

Next he requested Samuel to go with him to worship the Lord
and make things right, but Samuel refused. Samuel turned to
walk away from the King, but Saul grabbed his robe and it
tore. At this Samuel prophesied,

> *'The* LORD *has torn the kingdom of Israel from you today, and*
> *has given it to a neighbour of yours, who is better than you.'*
>
> (1 Samuel 15:28)

Immediately the idol of Saul's heart rose up within him and
demanded attention. He said to the prophet,

> *'I have sinned;* **yet honour me now, please, before the**
> **elders of my people and before Israel** *...'*
>
> (1 Samuel 15:30, my emphasis)

There it is again! The people! Notice Saul's type of repentance.
'I have sinned,' he said. Then in the next breath he begged for
honour because *what would the people say?* He said, 'Honour
me now, please, before the people. Yes, I have sinned but

don't humiliate me. Don't take away my honour. Do not take my peace away.'

Do Not Take Away Our Peace

I have been to some churches where the preaching brought conviction to the people and they began to cry out for mercy because of their sin. Then the pastor has said, 'Come on! Hallelujah, rejoice! We must rejoice because we are under grace. We are saved by grace and are going to heaven, come what may!'

When the Holy Spirit comes and convicts of sin, there will certainly be grief and people may feel dejected, but that is OK! God is actually working deeply in their lives. It defeats the purpose, therefore, when a man of God quenches the Spirit by saying, 'Hallelujah! We must not get sad about our spiritual state.' In other words, 'Quench the conviction, quench the Holy Spirit, please. We need our peace more than anything, even more than God!' Ease and convenience have become our idols, and many preachers faithfully shepherd God's people into this idolatry. That type of leadership is nothing but enmity to the souls of God's people.

And then you find the same leader at another time saying, 'Let us pray for revival.' What kind of revival will that be without the conviction of the Holy Spirit?

Beloved, if we want to continue playing church, that is OK, but if we want revival, we have got to make a choice. I know most Christians sincerely believe they are living for God, but the question is, how much are we *not living for God*? And if we are not living for God in certain areas, then for whom are we living? Can two walk together unless they agree (Amos 3:3)? Will God use us to transform our communities if we cannot even agree with Him concerning our own lives?

Self-esteem

A deeper examination of Saul's character reveals that his idol was really the love of his own reputation and image *before the people.* This desire for cheap popularity is a very common human weakness. He was so obsessed with his image before the people that he would do anything to remain in their high esteem. The reason he offered a sacrifice that he was not qualified to offer, was because he could not bear the thought of losing the trust and confidence of the people. He chose to disobey God by allowing the people to do what they wanted in contradiction of God's instruction, because he feared losing their favour.

Worst of all, at the moment of repentance which calls for humility, Saul demanded to be honoured *before the people and not forced to lose face* before them. It is this same idolatry that led him to resent David for being more popular than him. He ended up hunting down David to kill him, a mission he pursued for the rest of his life. He disregarded all the signs that showed that God's favour was with David and that David posed no threat to him. Many times he confessed his sin only to return to it again. He slipped further and further from the Lord until he lost the Spirit of God and was possessed by an evil spirit. Later he ended up having to consult witches for guidance. He could no longer hear from God (1 Samuel 28:7–8).

What About Us?

How many of us also disobey God because we don't want to be unpopular? How many times do we perform the same kind of acts of disobedience as Saul, because we do not want to antagonise people, wilfully holding back from obeying God if we sense that people may not approve?

Your life may be a huge scandal as far as God is concerned, even though you retain your position in the Church or ministry, but one day down the road it will all come tumbling out into the open. There was a pastor in England who knew for a long time that God wanted him to move in a particular direction. There were things God wanted him to do and things he was to let go of. I spoke to him some years back and told him that God wanted to use him, but he always excused himself because 'the parish would not allow it. What would the parishioners think? What would people say?' Since the parish employed him, he was worried about what the people would say, and feared that they would not move with God. Later, things got so bad in the parish that he had to resign, and has since started his own ministry.

Beloved, there are times when we fail God, not because we are incapable of doing right but because of the people around us and the society we live in. The subtle part of the deception is that, in spite of our failures, we are happy to report that we are obeying God! We argue that God understands that we are doing our best; therefore He does not really mind even when we deliberately choose to act contrary to His commands by honouring people before Him. We do not realise how much our world system has got the better of us. Our world is dictating what we can and cannot do for God. But this is not so much because the world is too powerful for us to resist; rather it is because there are things we love more than we love the Lord, and the world conveniently seems to offer them to us.

With this kind of understanding and compromise in today's Church, most of us do not regard the offences of King Saul as particularly grave. We see that in each instance he allowed the right thing to be done but with some compromise in the details, and to us that does not really matter because we too do it every day. Most of us know God has called us to be something in our individual lives and to play an important role in the lives of people in our families, cities and nations, but in many cases we have failed because of our compromised obedience. And this is usually because there are things that matter to us more than God. It is a sad truth and one that most people will not readily admit, but the fruits of our lives tell it all.

Saul and David Compared

David, like Saul, was anointed king by the prophet Samuel. He was also a human being like each one of us and had his own weaknesses. He failed and sinned in a way that most of us would find very difficult to forgive. Actually to our modern minds, David did more hideous things than Saul. It is therefore puzzling to see the ease with which David secured God's forgiveness while Saul failed.

But the most important thing to note here is that while Saul was obsessed with his image before people, David seemed to care more about his image before God. It is written about him that he was a man after God's heart (cf. 1 Samuel 13:14). When he was confronted by the prophet Nathan about his sin, he did not try to play it down or deny it.

Saul's self-image was a big deal. However, when David was accused by the prophet Nathan of sin in the case of Bathsheba, he went and began to fast and pray and seek God. All Israel knew about the great sin he had committed, but he didn't try to hide it. He openly repented. His servants begged him, 'Please, King, eat something. Don't keep beating yourself up!' But he wouldn't listen to them. He focused on God.

Yes, you are a child of God. Yes, God has chosen you. Yes, God has called you. But these truths do not necessarily mean that you are all right. Should you continue the way you are?

Is the Holy Spirit Really with Us?

God deals with us in seasons and there are times when He tells us, 'Let's move on.' If we don't move with Him at that particular time, we could end up like Saul who eventually resorted to consulting a witch because God had moved on and left him behind.

Even after the Spirit of the Lord had left Saul, he remained king for years. People saw and treated him as king. They didn't see anything different but, nevertheless, God had left him. Not only did the Holy Spirit leave Saul, but a demonic spirit started tormenting him. People around him wondered what to do and eventually brought David to minister to him. Even that, however, could not restore him. He sank deeper and deeper under satanic oppression.

Many false doctrines come into the Church because people reach the same point as Saul. At one particular point in time, perhaps God speaks to individuals instructing them to change, but they fail to act and eventually they reach the place where they want to walk in the power of God but they cannot, and so they try to conjure up something to prove that God is still with them. On the outside they still appear every inch a genuine Christian. Once in a while they attend conferences and experience some kind of relief, but they are not completely restored. That seed of bondage remains in their lives. In the end they begin to criticise anointed and functional ministries, finding fault with everything in order to try to justify themselves.

Saul reached that place of no longer moving under the anointing, and attempted to destroy those with the anointing (David) because he did not deal with his problem. He rejected God's counsel and ended up in a place where God would not speak to him anymore.

Proverbs 1:23–28 says,

'If you had responded to my rebuke,
I would have poured out my heart to you
and made my thoughts known to you.
But since you rejected me when I called
and no one gave heed when I stretched out my hand,
since you ignored all my advice
and would not accept my rebuke,
I in turn will laugh at your disaster;
I will mock when calamity overtakes you –
when calamity overtakes you like a storm,
when disaster sweeps over you like a whirlwind,
when distress and trouble overwhelm you.
Then they will call to me but I will not answer;
they will look for me but will not find me.'   (NIV)

Beloved, let us not be deceived. God cannot be mocked. What we sow we shall reap. Saul was anointed king of God's people, a prophet used by God, and yet he ended up consulting a witch to tell him what God was saying. Even the witch asked him, 'What do you want from me?' The time will come when the world will say to the Church, 'What are you believers seeking from us? Why are you coming to us for help?'

Joseph

Joseph was another man set apart for God's use to accomplish a divine mission. Genesis 49:26 says about Joseph:

> *'The blessings of your father*
> *Have excelled the blessings of my ancestors,*
> *Up to the utmost bound of the everlasting hills.*
> *They shall be on the head of Joseph,*
> *And on the crown of the head of him who was*
> > ***separate from his brothers.'***   (my emphasis)

Note the phrase *'separate from his brothers'*. Deuteronomy 33:16b repeats the same words:

> *'Let the blessing come "on the head of Joseph,*
> *And on the crown of the head of him who was*
> > *separate from his brothers." '*

Joseph was his father Jacob's favourite child. As a young boy, God showed Joseph visions of the calling upon his life, and Joseph shared the visions with his relatives. Unfortunately – or fortunately perhaps – the relatives didn't receive them very well. His father didn't believe him and his brothers became envious. It was an environment in which God's purpose for Joseph's life could not come to pass. Joseph needed to be separated from that environment in order to be prepared for God's calling on his life. He needed to be set apart and, in the process, he lost everything he prized and trusted in.

The first thing he lost was the security of his family. He was sold into slavery. He was taken out of his comfort zone, the

culture of his family, the norms he was used to, into a land
with a different culture, language, lifestyle, etc. In Egypt,
where he was taken, Joseph had to drop the values and
attitudes he had acquired from his family. He had to begin
life afresh. The pride of family connections vanished.

Potiphar, an official of Pharaoh the King of Egypt, bought
Joseph. Soon Joseph became Potiphar's favourite servant, just
as he had been his father's favourite child. He prospered in
Potiphar's house. It was not long, however, before he found
himself in prison, by God's appointment. God was taking
away dependence on his natural abilities which had enabled
him to become Potiphar's favourite. No, the devil didn't cast
Joseph into prison. God did!

In prison, Joseph used the spiritual gifts God had given him.
He started interpreting dreams and prophesying. Even those
gifts, however, didn't immediately get him out of prison. He
spent years in jail with his gifts. God wanted him to learn not
even to depend on God-given spiritual gifts.

Finally, after years of God working deeply within Joseph, he
was set apart and ready for God's use. He was ready to rule. As
Joseph stood before Pharaoh, he had nothing to boast of in
himself. Asked how he was able to interpret Pharaoh's dream,
Joseph said: *'It is not in me; God will give Pharaoh an answer
of peace'* (Genesis 41:16). All Joseph had at that time was
God. His God. No confidence in his human abilities, family
connections or even spiritual gifts.

Years later, Joseph was reunited with his family but, by that
point, he was such a different man that they could not change
him. Instead, he was in position to change them, and he did.
He was a man set apart for God's use.

God had told Abraham that his descendants would go into
slavery in a foreign country (Genesis 15:13). To fulfil that
prophecy, God set Joseph apart and used him. For a while God
will let us get on with the things we set ourselves to do, but
there comes a time when God says, 'Come apart and be
separate. You've seen that I am real. You've proved My faithfulness. I have given you a calling. But now come apart and I

will you show how to make things happen My way. Let Me do a work in you and then I will use you in the nations.'

Moses

God told Abraham that his descendants would go into slavery for four hundred years but then He would set them free and take them back to the land of Canaan. When the time came for deliverance, God chose a man and set him apart for the task.

Moses was brought up in Pharaoh's palace. He was in line to become Pharaoh himself. He knew everything about Egypt: lifestyle, attitudes, world view. By human standards and in the worldly sense, he was a man destined for greatness. Moses had a calling on his life to deliver the Israelites and he knew it. The desire to see his people set free was burning in him like a fire. He was full of zeal. In fact, his human zeal made him kill a man in an attempt to deliver his people. However, as long as Moses had so much of Egypt in him, God could not use him. He had first to be set apart from the things he had learnt to value and trust in.

God used the incident of the murder of the Egyptian to get Moses away from Egypt and for forty years he was alone in the land of Midian as a fugitive. When he went back to stand before Pharaoh as God's man, Moses had nothing of Egypt in or about him. He was a changed man, set apart for God. God had now anointed him with authority, not only over Egypt, but also as a shepherd over Israel.

Joshua

For most of the forty years that Israel wandered in the wilderness, while everyone slept in their tents, Joshua spent his days and nights in the Lord's tent. Whenever Moses went into the tent to speak to the Lord, Joshua was there. When Moses went out to the people, Joshua remained in the tent with the Lord. When Moses went up the mountain to seek

God, Joshua accompanied him. He never saw or experienced God like Moses, but he was there.

When Moses died, Joshua was God's natural choice of a successor. God told him in effect, 'Joshua, you who have set yourself apart for Me for so long, arise, because I will use you to bring My people into the land I've promised them.'

Daniel and the Three Hebrews

Daniel, Meshach, Shadrach and Abednego were among the captives carried away from Judah by Nebuchadnezzar, the King of Babylon. The Babylonian king, though a heathen, knew the concept of being set apart. He commanded that some young men from among the captives, including the four mentioned above, be taken, set apart and trained in the science and skills of Babylon. During their period of training they were to eat the same food as the king. After three years, they were to be presented before the king.

However, the Bible says, *'Daniel purposed in his heart that he would not defile himself with the portion of the king's delicacies, nor with the wine which he drank . . . '* (Daniel 1:8). This was true also of the other three Hebrew boys. They refused to adhere to the Babylonian dietary system. They set themselves apart for God even though they were captives, believing that God would honour their faith and commitment. The result was that God used them to challenge the wisdom and mindset of the Babylonians. God gave them authority over the land of their captivity, with Daniel ending up as Prime Minister.

John the Baptist

The Lord showed me that all the people whom He mightily used, both in the Old and New Testaments, were set apart. When God wanted to introduce a new era, a new phase in His dealings with humankind, John the Baptist was set apart to bring about this fundamental change. The Messiah was coming.

The Baptist was set apart even before he was born. When the time came for him to embark on his ministry, he went into the wilderness and, without any form of advertisement, multitudes went out to hear him and be baptised by him. The people were not attracted to John because he was a refined preacher. Neither did they come because his message was soothing to the ears. The Baptist preached a message of judgement and repentance. He was not even polite in his preaching, as his denouncement of the religious elite as a 'brood of vipers' clearly illustrates (see Matthew 3:7).

In the natural there was no reason why anyone would leave the high life of Jerusalem and go and seek out John in the barren wilderness. His secret was that he was a man set apart. Jesus Himself said that, among all born of women, there had never lived a greater man than John the Baptist (Matthew 11:11).

The Apostles

In his Gospel, Mark writes, referring to the Lord Jesus,

> *'And He went up on the mountain and called to Him those He Himself wanted. And they came to Him. Then He appointed twelve, that they might be with Him and that He might send them out to preach, and to have power to heal sicknesses and to cast out demons.'* (Mark 3:13–15)

After the Lord had spent a night in prayer, He called twelve of His disciples to Himself. Note that He did not call them to ministry or to a club, but to *Himself*. The purpose for this call was, first and foremost, that the twelve might be *'with Him'*. Later on, they were sent out to preach.

The twelve were all grown-up men who had jobs and families, and their own lifestyles. The Lord wanted to use them to preach the gospel but, first, they had to be set apart from the rest of the crowds that followed Him. That was why He called them to be with Him. To respond to this call, they had to forego their lifestyle. They had to discard their attitudes and world view. They could not go wherever they wanted anymore.

After the Lord's death and resurrection, He met them and told them, *'tarry in the city of Jerusalem until you are endued with power from on high'* (Luke 24:49). They were now ready to be anointed with power and authority. They were ready to be sent out to preach. According to Acts 4:13, the apostles had such boldness and authority that the Sanhedrin *'took note that these men had been with Jesus'* (NIV).

The Apostle Paul

Paul had a tremendous experience on the road to Damascus (Acts 9). He had a powerful encounter with the Lord, during which he heard the voice of the Lord. A few days later, he was filled with the Holy Spirit and experienced a personal miracle of healing when Ananias laid hands on him. He then began preaching immediately.

Maybe you are one of those who say, 'I have the Holy Spirit. I know what you're talking about. When the Holy Spirit came upon me, God set me apart.' Paul was filled with the Holy Spirit and began to preach but the process of being set apart was just beginning.

Paul had studied the Pentateuch thoroughly and so he knew the Scriptures. He had the information to prove that Jesus was indeed the Christ promised in the Old Testament. From Damascus, Paul went to Jerusalem and preached while staying with the apostles, the leaders of the Church, the men who had been with Jesus physically. He became a disciple of the big names.

You would have thought that with such a background – spectacular conversion, filled with the Holy Spirit, personal miracle of healing, keeping company with the leaders of the Church – God would have started using Paul immediately. Not quite. God had a purpose and a calling for Paul – to break down the barrier between Jew and Gentile by taking the gospel to the Gentiles. But first he had to be set apart so that God could work within him deeply. Consequently, just when it appeared as if things were beginning to fall in place, persecution arose and Paul had to leave Jerusalem in a hurry, rejected.

For years after that, Paul was hidden from public view. Nobody knows what he was doing all that time. He surfaced again in Antioch, having been sought out by Barnabas, and he joined the ministry team there. One day as the leaders of the church in Antioch, the teachers and the prophets, were fasting and ministering to the Lord (these were men given to seeking God as a lifestyle), the Holy Spirit said, *'Set apart for me Barnabas and Saul for the work to which I have called them'* (Acts 13:2). And so the two men were set apart. I don't know how it was done but they did it. The leaders then continued seeking God. Much later, Paul and Barnabas went out preaching.

Several years later, Paul wrote to the Galatians that God had led him into the desert of Arabia where he had spent three years, alone with God. It was there that he was given the deep revelations he taught. God worked deeply in him. When he came back from there, he was a new man, changed forever. Like Moses, Paul met with God personally. He had an extended encounter with the Lord, during which a deep work was done in his life.

Beloved, when God sets you apart for a season and works deeply in you, you come out totally different from those who live by the norm. Your heart is different, your rules are different, and your world view is different. You don't fear what they fear. What they yearn for has no appeal to you. What they esteem is abominable to you. *You are different.*

If we are going to make an impact, we have got to reach that moment when we make the decision to set ourselves apart for God, that He may work in our lives that which we cannot work in ourselves; that He may make us what we cannot make ourselves. God will then separate us from things that we cannot separate ourselves from and use us to reflect His glory.

Momentarily, my mind went back to November 1988 when the Lord spoke to me through the late Apostle Deo Balabye-kubbo, that if I would go into the wilderness and be apart, He would speak to me. Through a series of occurrences, I found myself away from Kampala city for a whole year and it was during that period that the Lord visited me and gave me a calling and the anointing to fulfil it.

Chapter 5

Nazirites

Following the terrorist attacks, I couldn't leave America for about a week because all the airports were shut down. When I finally managed to travel, I went to Austria where I continued seeking God, asking Him to teach me more.

One morning, while I was reading the Bible, the Lord brought to my attention the word 'Nazirite'. It is a word that does not occur very often in the Bible, and until that time I thought I knew everything about it. I looked it up in the Bible package on my computer to see what it really means. I found out that the word is spelt in one of two ways: Nazarite (with 'a') or Nazirite (with 'i'). This is because the word has two Hebrew roots. One is the Hebrew root word *Nazir* (from which 'Nazirite' comes), which means 'set apart for God, sanctified, consecrated to reflect God's glory'. In essence, *Nazir* means 'removed from common standards in order to meet the standard of God'. The second Hebrew root word is *Nazar* (from which we get the word 'Nazarite'), which has a similar meaning: 'elevated above others, set apart, given authority over the land'. Combined, the two Hebrew words speak of 'being set apart, purified, being made to reflect the glory of God, raised above the norm and given authority over the nation'.

Through my study I discovered that the Nazirites in the Bible came to the fore when the nation of Israel or individuals encountered situations that were beyond their human ability to deal with – situations that were so impossible that they could not handle them on their own. During such times, people took vows to set themselves apart for God, to live as Nazirites for a time.

Three Categories of Nazirites

There were three categories of Nazirites. In the first were people who, out of their own free will, set themselves apart for a season. These were temporary Nazirites. In the second were those who were made Nazirites by other people, e.g. Samuel was made a Nazirite by his mother Hannah. In the third category were Nazirites who were chosen by God Himself, not self-chosen or chosen by parents. They were born Nazirites and had to live as such all of their lives. Examples are John the Baptist and Samson, whom God set apart from before they were born. Much higher discipline was required of such people, and they usually had great impact.

The Lord Jesus spoke of eunuchs (see Matthew 19). He said that some were born eunuchs, some were made eunuchs by others, and some chose to be eunuchs for the kingdom of God. Eunuchs were people who were separated from others in order to serve certain purposes. For example, they did not marry like everyone else. Eunuchs lived the principles of the Nazirite lifestyle.

People who became temporary Nazirites did so for various reasons. We see examples of these in the Acts of the Apostles. Some were motivated by zeal for God, while others who were seeking a solution to insurmountable problems embarked upon a period of separation to seek God and draw close to Him. Permanent Nazirites remained that way mainly because of the call of God upon their lives.

Nazirite Lifestyle

People who lived as Nazirites had to take vows to observe certain rules and regulations. One of those rules was that they had to cut off their hair at the beginning of the period of separation and were not allowed to cut it again until it ended, regardless of how long their hair grew. They also vowed not to drink anything intoxicating, nor to touch anything dead or ritually unclean.

Each of the rules the Nazirites observed had a spiritual implication. For example, by abstaining from alcoholic drinks, the Nazirites were implying that nothing else apart from God would control their lives. Determining not to touch or eat anything unclean was a way of reiterating their total resolve to live a holy life of obedience to God.

Understandably, Nazirites had to exercise a great deal of self-control. They couldn't live like everyone else. They weren't free to do a lot of things. It sounds almost like bondage, but the result was that they experienced and brought about great deliverances.

Samson

Judges chapter 13 contains the record of the birth of Samson at a time when the nation of Israel was in captivity to the Philistines because of their sins. It was in fact God who had handed them over to their enemies. For forty years, they were tormented politically, physically and economically, with no ability to set themselves free.

There are times when we enter into bondage because of our own sins, foolishness, weakness or carelessness. At other times, we may find ourselves in bondage because of circumstances beyond our control; for example, we may be part of a wicked generation. When we are thus bound, we can't progress. We are limited by all kinds of hindrances.

God sent an angel to a barren woman, Manoah's wife, a victim of the prevailing judgement on the nation, telling her that she had been chosen by God to give birth to a child who would deliver Israel. But the angel gave her a warning:

> *'Now therefore, please be careful not to drink wine or similar drink, and not to eat anything unclean. For behold, you shall*

conceive and bear a son. And no razor shall come upon his head, for the child shall be a Nazirite to God from the womb; and he shall begin to deliver Israel out of the hand of the Philistines.'   (Judges 13:4–5)

God needed a Nazirite, a set-apart person, to deliver Israel. This wasn't a task to be undertaken by just any person. It needed someone consecrated, sold out to God. Samson was set apart from birth but unfortunately he messed up his calling by walking in ways that compromised him.

Samuel

Samuel was consecrated as a Nazirite by his mother. When Hannah asked God for Samuel, she made a vow:

'O LORD of hosts, if You will indeed look on the affliction of Your maidservant and remember me, and not forget Your maidservant, but will give Your maidservant a male child, then I will give him to the LORD all the days of his life, and no razor shall come upon his head.'   (1 Samuel 1:11)

The vows Hannah made were Nazirite vows. God honoured Hannah's vows and so Samuel was born a Nazirite. And yes, he did reflect the glory of God: people saw God in him; he had authority over the nation. Although he lived in a generation which, the Bible tells us, was very wicked, the boy Samuel ministered before God. He was a Nazirite, set apart from the rest.

John the Baptist

John the Baptist was a Nazirite. Before he was born the angel told his father Zechariah that he would be set apart for God, tasting nothing intoxicating and being filled with the Holy Spirit from birth (see Luke 1:11ff.).

Apostle Paul

The Apostle Paul took vows to live as a temporary Nazirite at least twice (Acts 18:18 and 21:23–26). When things got tough for Paul in his ministry, he made a vow and took time off to set himself apart. No wonder God used him so mightily.

Nazirite Principle

We do not have to take the Nazirite vow today in the very same way that people did in Bible days, but the principle of being set apart remains as necessary today as it was then. The minimum demand of God upon the Church is a people set apart for Him. We are in the world but we are not of the world (John 17:16). When God's people lose sight of this demand, they cast off restraint. They become careless, walking however they wish, and then they wonder why they don't see the promises of God coming to pass. They ask why they never operate in the anointing that they know is available for them.

We Must Change

Beloved, the days ahead are going to be very difficult. Opposition to godliness is going to increase. We won't manage if we remain the way we are today. At least I know I won't manage. Unless we move to the level of consecration to which God is calling us, we won't make it.

I don't know about you, but the Lord has been showing me how much His grace has been holding me. And yes, by grace it will always do so. But beloved, when God sounds a warning that we had better move from one point to another, and we resist, claiming that we trust His grace to hold us, we miss it. He is the owner of grace! We won't stand unless we make changes. The grace of God is available only for those who are in the right position to receive it. God is saying right now, 'Over there at the place of being set apart is where my grace will uphold you through the dangerous times ahead.'

As long as we are not where God wants us to be in our walk with Him, we cannot move forward. So many Christians are suffering in their bodies, finances, relationships, etc. Whole churches and even nations are in bondage to confusion, fear and other forms of oppression. There are limitations everywhere. We have prayed with no results. We have asked God to remove bad leaders from our governments, but He hasn't. We know what we want to see happen and we ask God to bring these things about, but He seems unreachable. Some of us are even questioning whether prayer works anymore.

Beloved, God is just as ready to answer our prayers today as He has always been. There is power in prayer and, in this ministry, we have always emphasised prayer. But I can tell you that there is a place where prayers alone do not avail. During the Old Testament days, people prayed in times of trouble, but that wasn't all. They also gave offerings. There were times when only sacrifices brought results. Today, we do not have to offer physical blood sacrifices but the principle remains the same. If we want to see results we have to offer our lives as living sacrifices (Romans 12:1), to set ourselves apart for God. There is no other way around this.

I believe God is telling us in and through the troubles we are encountering, that we aren't where we ought to be. Not all the problems we go through are brought by the devil. God directly permits some of them so that He can get our attention and make us understand how much we need Him.

Chapter 6

Procrastination and Distractions

While I was in Austria I did not share much about the message God had given me because it was still so fresh. I was still seeking God about it. From Austria, I flew to Israel. The evening I arrived, I discovered that Langton Gatsi, my friend and fellow minister from Zimbabwe, was also in the country but was leaving the following morning. We therefore agreed to fellowship together that evening. For three hours, we shared with each other what we were each hearing from God. It was basically the same: a call to be set apart.

When I arrived back in Uganda, for two days I shared a little bit on the message. I then travelled to Berlin with Michael Kimuli, my partner in the ministry. There the Lord asked me this question: 'Will you leave this city also before starting on the journey?'

Ever since the Lord had spoken to me, I had been analysing my life and marvelling at all the things I was discovering. I had only started the journey in my mind: I wasn't getting any further. I asked the Lord why it was so difficult to be set apart for Him. The Lord replied that I should beware of two things: procrastination and distractions.

I immediately understood why procrastination is an enemy of giving our best to the Lord. All of us who are sincere can testify that we have allowed procrastination to mess up our resolve to be serious about the things of God again and again. We make up our mind to spend time seeking God, and when we begin, we experience joy and peace. We are encouraged. As we go on, however, at some point, something crops up, maybe an 'emergency', a need for ministry or some other demand. So we quickly change our mind and tell God that we will get back to Him later. Would He please excuse us so that we can handle the emergency? Or maybe the Lord reveals something in our life that isn't right, and we tell Him that we will deal with it later.

But beloved, when we tell the Lord that we will deal later with the issues He is telling us to deal with now, we cannot continue enjoying our walk with Him. The anointing lifts off us. The presence of God goes. The joy goes. We may even continue seeking the Lord but as long as that issue is in our lives, our prayers will become cold, dry and empty. We may have our reasons why we feel we cannot face our sins and get them out of the way once and for all, but as long as we keep saying, 'Later, Lord. I will deal with it later!', it is almost as if God also says, 'And I will meet you later, too.'

If you are a minister of the gospel, sometimes the Lord may show you He wants you to move from one point to another within a certain period so that you will be prepared for a future ministry engagement in your diary. He knows that the people you are to minister to and the events you are to face require a special word from Him, and so you need to move to another level, you need to work on your life, you may need to let some things go. You know there is a time limit, and so you begin to plan to work on what God has pointed out to you. But then things happen that distract you and take your focus onto something completely different. You soon realise that you are not on track and you feel a sense of guilt. You say, 'Oh God, have mercy. Bear with me. Give me the strength, the grace. Tomorrow, Lord.' Sometimes you say, 'Lord, starting next week, I will change.' It goes on like that until suddenly you realise the engagement is for the following day and you have not worked upon your life as God wanted.

You go and keep the engagement. Outwardly, you are a very faithful minister. You keep your appointment. The people see a man or woman of God but they don't know what you are going through on the inside. As you mount the pulpit, you whisper a desperate prayer: 'God, I have let you down. Forgive me. But please, Lord, it is not about me. For the sake of Your people, stretch forth Your hand. Please work. I promise that as soon as I finish this I will start on the journey.' Sometimes you stand up there and God does His work nevertheless, and you breathe a sigh of relief: 'Thank You, Lord. Where would I be without Your loving-kindness?'

This does not just happen to gospel ministers. You could be a businessperson, a housewife, or whoever. You know that God is saying, 'Move on. I want to use you. I want to change your world through you', and within you, you really want to do it. You know it is the best thing for you. You know that if only you could move to that place in your life, you would be fulfilled. You make a resolution that you are going to obey. But then other things begin clamouring for your attention too. Pretty soon, you are bargaining with God: 'Lord, give me a little more time. I can't get started right now.' After a while, you begin to feel that maybe God is grieved. So you stop talking about it for some days. This goes on and on.

It is not that we don't love God. What I am describing is the situation of lives not being wholly yielded. We give, but not all of ourselves. We love, but not wholly. We don't love Him with *all* our heart. In word we say it and sometimes we convince ourselves that we mean what we say but when we are really honest with ourselves, we find it is not true.

Beloved, God will not let us go forward until we have dealt with the things He is showing us. Just when our devotional prayers are becoming deep and sweet, those issues will come back to our minds, and because we aren't willing to deal with them, our prayers die right there, as if a cold bucket of water is poured over us. Sometimes, we stop praying altogether for a while, or whenever we pray and the issues come to mind, we try to avoid mentioning anything about them.

We are all guilty of postponing the fulfilment of promises we have made to God. We have all at one time or another postponed acts of obedience the Lord was calling upon us to perform. The Lord tells us to take a fast, and we say, 'Not now, Lord; next month.' We actually bargain with the Lord to disobey Him: 'Lord, I know what Your will is. I know that this sin in my life is the reason why I am not doing well, but let me first solve a few problems. I will deal with what You are saying later. Please understand and bear with me, Lord!'

So we keep procrastinating. Sometimes, we keep postponing acts of obedience for years. Five years after the Lord first called upon us to get rid of something wicked in our life, we are still saying, 'Lord, later'. In the meantime, we pray but there are no breakthroughs. We tell God that we love Him but deep in our heart we know that we are lying. We may even try to use high-sounding words, maybe the English of the King James Version of the Bible, to try to impress God so that He doesn't remind us of the issues; or we may decide to keep our prayers superficial, avoiding going any deeper in case the issue comes up. In the meantime, no fellowship.

To make everything worse, the more we procrastinate, the harder our hearts become. By postponing obeying the Lord, we are quenching the voice of the Holy Spirit, the only voice who can lead us to repentance. As we keep pushing aside the conviction of the Holy Spirit, He too keeps going further and further away.

Thank God for His immeasurable patience. He never gives up on us, but how much we must hurt Him with our disobedience!

The Lord spoke to me that the reason I wasn't getting started on the journey was because I was procrastinating, promising to begin later. And the reason I was procrastinating was because I wasn't yet really willing to deal with the excuses for my disobedience. He showed me that unless I was ready to commit myself and die to the things holding me back, I would continue postponing the beginning of the journey.

Then He reminded me of the numerous times in the past when I had made plans to seek Him but then something else had come up and I had changed my plans. I had changed my focus. On other occasions, I had diverted what I had intended to give to the Lord. I could remember the times when I allowed visitors to cancel my plans to pray, etc.

The Lord showed me that those interruptions, genuine or non-genuine, were distractions. If I wanted to start on the journey of being set apart, I had to deal with distractions. I had to make a choice. I had to make up my mind, right then. As long as I kept allowing distractions to interrupt my plans, I would never make a start.

Chapter 7

Prison Gates

As I kept seeking the Lord, He showed me that the limitations and bondages that keep us from being set apart for God fall under three categories, namely sins that beset, our world and the works of the devil. I call these three categories our prison gates.

1. Sins that Beset

Hebrews 12:1 says,

> 'Wherefore, seeing we also are compassed about with so great a cloud of witnesses, let us lay aside every weight, and the sin which doth so easily beset us, and let us run with patience the race that is set before us.' (KJV)

The sins that beset us are those sins that have been in our lives for so long that they have become part of us, part of our personalities. Entire portions of our lives are dedicated to them. Often we set aside a time to engage in them daily. These are sins we do not fall into, but rather walk in. They are a part of our thinking, our speech and our attitudes. We engage in these sins without any feelings of guilt, though at the back of our minds we know that they are contrary to God's Word.

And these sins aren't always necessarily what we consider to be 'big' or scandalous commissions. They could be one of those so-called 'harmless' habits, or even omissions – not doing what we know we ought to do. Regardless of whether they are 'big' or 'small', sins that beset mess up our love for Christ, stealing joy, peace and victory out of our lives. We cannot hope to go far with the Lord, to walk in His authority and power, when we are habitually, knowingly, sinning against Him without even feeling any guilt. Sin remains sin whether we condone it or not, and God, the Holy God, will not work closely with us so long as we walk deliberately in sin.

The sins that easily beset us usually have their hold on our minds. In our minds we come to accept them as being part of us. Sometimes, we even become proud of them, because, we claim, they are what make our personalities different from others'! The sins shape and control our attitudes.

An example of this kind of sin is racism. Generally, we Christians know that racism is ungodly. But if individuals have a bias against another race, the moment they encounter a person of that race, without even thinking, they immediately become negative. Their emotions rise up, their facial expressions change and ultimately whatever they do or say to that other person of a different race will be negative. It all happens so effortlessly. The problem is in the mindset.

Another example is lust, when individuals accept it as a part of them. The moment they see a person of the opposite sex or, in some cases, of the same sex (homosexuals), unconsciously and effortlessly, they get fired up with immoral desire.

Beloved, God is saying we must be set apart from all sin if we are to walk with Him in the difficult days ahead. We must examine ourselves in order to identify the sins that beset us and resolve to deal with them once and for all. Many Christians will already have overcome these sins at some point in their Christian lives but now they are back again. They didn't return all of a sudden. They came back slowly, and because we didn't resist them, they are once again strongly embedded in us. We call them *our* problems, *our* sins, *our* weaknesses. We pray, 'Lord, You know my problem. There is nothing I can do about it.' That is a lie. We can do something about any sin. If we couldn't, the Lord wouldn't tell us to get rid of it. We must face up to those sins, repent and be set apart for God.

2. Our World

One other reason why we are the way we are, why we act the way we do and why we live the way we live, is because of the worlds we belong to. When we talk about the world, many of us immediately think of immorality, drunkenness and all the usual vices. But I am talking about our world in the sense of the systems around us. Our worlds are made up of our families, workplaces, friends, acquaintances and responsibilities.

The parable of the sower gives a clear warning about the danger of being caught up in the world:

> *'Now he who received seed among the thorns is he who hears the word, and the cares of this world and the deceitfulness of riches choke the word, and he becomes unfruitful.'*
>
> (Matthew 13:22)

Jesus told us that, even though we are in the world, we are not to be of the world. To be of the world is to 'belong', to be in the world's power, to be under its influence. Our environment, the people we live among, the traditions and customs of the societies we live in, our culture: these things that make up our worlds are many times hindrances to us giving ourselves totally to the Lord.

You want to go on with God, but how will it affect your family, your job and your friends? You want to obey God financially, to order your finances according to God's principles, but how can you be sure that you will survive in this corrupt environment? You want to change your ways, to conform to God's standard, but what will people say when they see you doing things differently from everybody else? And so you pray, 'Lord, I want to be set apart for You but I cannot, because my world won't allow it.'

Often even our acts of service to God, our 'religion', may form part of that world that hinders our being wholly the Lord's. For example, the Lord may be calling upon you to spend time with Him in prayer but you say you can't because you have to go to choir practice or to a church board meeting. Your world is made up of church work, giving you no time for God Himself. You put the expectations that church people have of you above God's call to be with Him. You now gain your identity from your world of religious service instead of from Christ.

You might be a pastor of a Charismatic church. You sense that what you are is not what you want to be and you are conscious you are not being all you want to be. There are things God is pointing out to you. God is showing you that He wants to move you to new levels in Him. God may be telling you to stop what you are doing and move on to something else, or to take time off and seek His face. You know very well what you ought to do, but at the same time you are confronted with the demands of the church. So you say, 'Oh God, what will happen to the church if I am not there? I can't leave now. Oh God, one of these days I will start.' The church is your world. As good as the task of taking care of the church is, it can become the reason for not excelling for the One you are trying to serve.

Your world includes your workplace, your ministry, your city and sometimes your country. In some countries, unless as a minister of the gospel you are willing to be radical, the kingdom of God will never advance. All the people agree about certain lifestyles and mindsets. They flow together in the atmosphere created by their culture and they are under the power of the spiritual influences that control that culture. Many may not believe in spiritual warfare. In their corporate agreement, they shut God out of their lives and open up to someone else: the enemy. That is how corporate bondage comes in. Whole cities and nations come under similar bondage. The spiritual territory that the people have denied God, is taken over by the power of darkness. An evangelist may come to the city and preach the gospel but the people are so blinded and dulled that they cannot respond. The spiritual vacuum has been filled by the power of darkness and where there is darkness, there is blindness.

Beloved, there is a price to pay to walk with God. It has always been that way. When God called Abraham, He told him to get out of his world – his family, his society and his environment. Abraham could have asked how he and his family were going to survive in a strange land, among strange people. He could have said to God, 'At least show me the land itself first before I move my family there.' There were many reasons why Abraham could have chosen to stay on in his world. Abraham, however, chose to trust God, to surrender. Yes, when you decide to set yourself apart from your world, there will be pressures. There will be earthquakes, but those who persevere to the end will be saved (Matthew 24).

Our worlds control our mindsets and attitudes. Our worlds work to strengthen the sins of our lives. For example, if I am engaging in a particular sin, my world will provide me with friends who will help make me comfortable in my prison. They will encourage me to go on sinning. And so through the group support, as we encourage and aid one another, we create a system, a culture of our own. We create an atmosphere around us in which our sins can flow. Within this environment, we develop values, methods of acquiring wealth, rules governing relationships, etc. Eventually, we become so programmed to and by our world that we no longer struggle with the sins that beset us. We have the strength and support of our world. We are anchored to that world. We are part of it and it is part of us.

Being set apart from our world isn't easy because we have been programmed mentally and even physically to fit into it. We glide through that world effortlessly. It is costly leaving that world. Only people who determine to walk with God will pay the price. To become set apart from your world, you may have to give up some of your friends. A lot of things may have to change around you.

Now, being set apart doesn't mean we have to run away from people or anything like that. We can be set apart for God even when we are physically in an ungodly environment. Samuel grew up in the temple environment right where the sons of Eli were perpetuating extreme wickedness, but Samuel remained pure, set apart.

An Example of Our World's Control

A friend of mine, who lives in Berlin, Germany, attended a conference in Switzerland that greatly impacted her life. She was charged with so much fire for evangelism that she said to God, 'If You will put upon me the anointing and ability to bring people into the kingdom, I am going to witness everywhere.' In answer to her prayer, an anointing poured upon her and she had no doubt that she had received what she desired.

She travelled back home to Berlin full of faith, zeal and confidence, and immediately asked God for the souls of all the people living in her flats. When she got into the lift to take her luggage up to her apartment, someone else got into the lift as well. The Holy Spirit immediately prompted her to minister to that person. She thought, 'Hey, I have hardly got back into my apartment. Not now, Lord.' So she didn't say a single word.

The next morning she was praying, asking God to send a soul her way. The response was, 'How are you going to win people if you aren't going to talk?' She asked for forgiveness and promised to talk next time. After her time of prayer, she met two young boys in the lift. She made some small talk with the boys and then one of them said that his brother was sick. When my friend offered to pray for the sick child, the boys readily agreed even though they were not Christians. She laid hands on them there in the lift, prayed, and the boys left. That evening when she got home, the boys met her and thanked her for her prayer because the sick child had recovered the moment she had prayed. Full of joy, she entered her apartment and prayed, 'Lord, I promise that I am going to live for

You.' A few days later, she met the mother of the boy who had been healed and, after she had shared simply with her, the woman gave her life to Christ.

For about two months, she talked to a number of people, and three came to the Lord. Then it started happening: her job as a secretary slowly began to take her mind away from witnessing. She would come back home too tired to witness. Four months down the road, the passion and zeal were gone. She still met people whom she knew needed help, but somehow she just couldn't bring herself to do the right thing.

She related her experience to me and asked me, 'Why did God allow me to lose that zeal, passion and anointing when He knew I really wanted it?' I told her that her world was not programmed for ministry of that sort. She had tried to live her life as she had always done, in a 'normal' way, even after she had received the new anointing. She had continued living out her life as a normal secretary, giving time to all the people around her, going on holiday, etc., on top of trying to squeeze in this ministry of God. The result was that her world squeezed the anointing of God out of her life.

I told her that, when she took on this new mission in her life, she should have set new priorities. She should have cut certain things out of her life in order to maintain the anointing. I explained to her that she should have realised that there was no way she could keep living as she had always lived and still operate under that anointing.

That lady is a friend of many powerful ministers. She told me about a man of God from Argentina who is very anointed. Although he is a businessman as well as a great minister, he does not struggle. Signs and wonders follow his ministry. She had worked with him for a number of weeks and, in times of prayer for people's needs, he had asked her to join him in ministering to the people. She had laid hands on people and they had been healed and delivered so easily. In between ministry sessions, she had sat with the man of God, going over Scriptures, worshipping and rejoicing in the Lord.

When the time had come for the man of God to leave, she had said to him, 'It is so bad that you are going away. I love this life of miracles, signs and wonders. What will I do without you?' The man had scolded her for being silly since the Bible says all believers have authority. He had told her just to believe the Word. Upon her request, he had prayed for her to receive anointing.

The following day, she had ministered in a small fellowship and the anointing had been just as strong as when she had been with the man of God. Whenever she had been given opportunity to minister, the Holy Spirit had moved with mighty signs and wonders. Things went well for about six months and then, nothing. No more miracles. No more fire. No matter what she had tried, nothing had happened.

I explained that the problem was her world. During the time she had been in fellowship with the man of God, they had sought God together and that was why she had operated under the same anointing as him. As for her, she had not regarded those times of discussion and worship as anything special – just a nice time talking about the things of God. Her life had never been programmed to live with God at the level at which she could have that anointing on her perpetually. I told my sister that she needed to re-examine and re-evaluate her priorities.

Beloved, the way we live our lives is not programmed for revival. If it were, we would be revived by now. Most of us are captives of the world, obeying the dictates of routines and systems around us. If we are to set ourselves apart for God, we need to rethink our priorities.

Every person that has ever been used in revival has had to break free from the world around them, so that they could be yoked to God, married to His purposes. We are in the world but we must not be of the world. Everyone has a world, but we must remember that one day we will pass out of that world and the only thing that will matter then will be our fruit in the Lord. We must make up our minds that we are going to be set apart. Once that is done and we begin walking that road, no matter how rotten the world around us may be, we shall remain separated unto our God, Nazirites separated from others, purified to reflect the glory of God.

3. Works of the Devil

The third prison gate we face on this journey is the work of the devil. As we are all aware, the devil is at work in most of our lives wreaking one havoc or another. Now if we know that a particular hindrance we face in our journey to be set apart is clearly a work of Satan, then we must make up our minds, take our position, and tell the devil that enough is enough. Every work that is not consistent with the Word of God must be broken. We must not tolerate the blatant destruction caused by the devil. We are not meant to submit meekly to the devil's works. We are not meant to talk about how Satan is hindering and oppressing us, lamenting our situation. We have the legal right and ability to end Satan's activities in our bodies, families, finances, and so on. Let us arise and put a stop to the devil's activities. We know from 1 John 3:8 that the Son of God was manifested to destroy the works of the devil.

One aspect of the devil's attack is that he aims to limit us by unjustifiably inflicting evil upon us. But there is another aspect which is even more lethal: the devil works within us in such a way that he uses us to destroy one another. One of Satan's major strategies is to cause *woundedness*. Beloved, God's people are carrying within them many wounds which have been inflicted upon them by their fellow believers. As I travel around the world, I learn about people, their histories and wounds. I discover that there are things one cannot say in one nation about another nation. Wounds exist between nations resulting from long periods of injustice, prejudice, etc., and even believers carry them. For instance, people still suffer from and nurse the wounds of pain and anger inflicted upon them as nations by other nations during the Second World War.

I hear Christians make statements like, 'Don't tell me about those people', referring to believers of other nations or races.

They are Christians but the love of Christ has not penetrated their hearts in those particular areas.

These wounds limit us. We want to be the best for God that we can be, but they hold us back. They suppress the purpose of God in our lives. We want God to pour out His Holy Spirit but the Lord is looking at these things. Sometimes, we repent but we don't go deep enough because we are not aware that we are captives to the works of the enemy. We feel that to some extent we are justified for reacting in the way we do because, after all, we really were unjustifiably hurt. What we forget, however, is that it was not God who hurt us. It was the enemy who inspired the injustice. Instead of continuing to direct our hatred towards our fellow believers, we must recognise our true enemy.

We must stop focusing on our pain because all that does is make us give back poison, causing us to break the one commandment Jesus gave to us – *to love one another* (John 13:34). Jesus told us to love others as He has loved us. Does He love us because we are so perfect? No! The Bible says that when we were still His enemies, He loved us enough to die for us. So we have no ground to insist that we must maintain our animosities against others, nations or individuals, because they wrongly hurt us. We ourselves do not much deserve to be loved and appreciated by God. And if we think that it is impossible for us to love others the Bible way on our own, that is the very reason why God is calling us to set ourselves apart, so that He may work in us and separate us from the things that limit us.

I have talked to some very anointed men of God and heard them say things like, 'Oh, brother, those people need our prayers.' This kind of talk is a very subtle manifestation of pride. The real message is: 'They are not our class. We are way up here, the anointed ones. They are down there. No wonder they aren't going anywhere!' Pride is a terrible thing and we need God's help to stay clear of it. It is the most subtle sin in our lives. Nobody ever notices pride in their own lives. We need to keep each other accountable when we see pride.

When we act in a way that breaks relationships among people – slandering, gossiping and ruining others' reputations – aren't we actually working with and for the devil? The call to separate ourselves from Satan's works does not just require that we break free from satanic oppression, but also from acting in obedience to him. The kind of betrayal found among believers is alarming. We say we love God but right inside church buildings, or even during services, we deliberately castigate and destroy others' testimonies.

It is time to set ourselves apart. Beloved, time is running out. We can't continue playing games. We have to come out clearly and show whose side we are on: God's or the enemy's.

The Place of Grace

We talk of grace, and I do believe in grace, but, beloved, it is terrible for us to keep on in our own way until we have to hear God say, 'I have called and called to you but you refused, and now I won't have anything to do with you.' In the history of the Jews, there came a point when God said:

> *'But today I am freeing you from the chains on your wrists. Come with me to Babylon, if you like, and I will look after you; but if you do not want to, then don't come. Look, the whole country lies before you; go wherever you please.'*
> (Jeremiah 40:4 NIV)

My heart is grieved by some of the teachings about grace that are circulating today, wrongly insulating our spirits against sin. The God of the Bible is not that cheap. He is principled. I am talking about the teachings that say that grace will be there to the end. But if there is no repentance, sin continues to grow; when it reaches its fullness, it produces death. Grace is still there. It does not go away, and that is why when God sees sin reaching its fullness, He calls, 'Come back, come to Me. Come out of those things. I love you.' But if we do not listen, if we don't turn around, God cries and grieves as He watches sin cut us down. He loves us and longs to hold us to Himself and protect us from falling, but He can't violate His own principles. He has given us free will which means we have the choice either to receive His grace or walk away.

PART 2

The Process

Chapter 8

Surrender: The Starting Point

While in Berlin, the Lord gave me words of encouragement for all those who will decide to embark on the journey of being set apart. I was disgusted with myself and angry at the devil. I became so discouraged that I asked the Lord to allow me to come back to Uganda and just let me go hide in some obscure place for a long time. I was very ashamed at the way I had led a life of lies for so long.

Then the Lord led me to Isaiah 44:1–3:

> 'Yet hear now, O Jacob My servant,
> And Israel whom I have chosen.
> Thus says the LORD who made you
> And formed you from the womb, who will help you:
> "Fear not, O Jacob My servant;
> And you, Jeshurun, whom I have chosen.
> For I will pour water on him who is thirsty,
> And floods on the dry ground;
> I will pour My Spirit on your descendants,
> And My blessing on your offspring." '

He also gave me Isaiah 49:25:

> 'But thus says the LORD:
> "Even the captives of the mighty shall be taken away,
> And the prey of the terrible be delivered;
> For I will contend with him who contends with you,
> And I will save your children." '

When I read these words, I at first thought the Lord was trying to prepare me for the imminent opposition I would face as I obeyed the command to call the Church to be set apart. However, the Lord explained to me that the enemies He would contend with in my life were the limitations, bondages, etc., that were hindering my walk with Him. That encouraged me a great deal. I knew then that the Lord was not going to cast me away. I was encouraged to pursue the journey no matter what the cost. Then the Lord instructed me to share these same scriptures with His people everywhere.

Beloved, have you messed up your life? Have things gone very wrong in your life? Do you feel rotten because of all the sins you have committed? God the Father is saying to you personally that He has not given up on you! Yes, He sees and knows everything but He has no intention of casting you away. People may write you off but the Lord will never do so. He is for you, not against you.

There is another problem I have noticed with some leaders in the Church: they give the false impression that they as leaders are perfect, infallible, know it all and do it all; yet they themselves know very well that they do not walk according to the standards expected by God. And because those leaders insist that they aren't missing it anywhere, their followers are also led to lower their standards, and the fear of God is lost.

Beloved, we must all admit that we are human. None of us has got it all together. We are all on a pilgrimage. No one has arrived yet. God is not through with any of us yet. One of the greatest inspirations I have ever received to pursue a life of prayer came when I read a book written by Dr David Yonggi Cho, the pastor of the largest church in the world. In that book, Dr Cho shared how he sometimes struggles to pray. I was surprised to read that, because I had always thought that men and women of Dr Cho's spiritual stature did not have to struggle with such things as getting out of bed at night to pray. As I read the book, I shouted out loud, 'Lord, I am not the only one who struggles with prayer. Dr Cho does too, but the difference is that he overcomes. I also will overcome!'

So beloved, we are all on this journey together. Be encouraged. This journey is not only for some special people with extraordinary grace. Every one of us can be set apart.

Believe the Message

When the Lord called Abraham, if he had refused to believe the word God gave him, nothing would have happened! Yes, there were many unanswered questions but Abraham chose to believe the few words God spoke to him. The Bible does not say that God spoke to Abraham in some spectacular way. I don't know exactly how God spoke to him but it certainly was not in some loud, frightening voice, accompanied by earthquakes, etc. The impression I get is that the voice of God was simple, probably not very exciting. Obeying that kind of voice required faith.

Hebrew 11:6 says that it is impossible to please God without faith. In Seattle, the Lord asked me, 'Will you believe what I am telling you?' And I too ask every person reading this book: Will you believe that God is calling you personally to be set apart for Him?

You are not reading this book by accident. God wants you to receive this message. Will you? You can only do so by faith! Will you respond to the call God is sending out in these dangerous days?

Do Not Miss God

The message in this book is not another wonderful teaching for you to store in your bank of spiritual information. Either you are going to have to act on what God is saying, or, if you are going to reject the call of God, you might as well stop reading right here.

I am aware that for some readers it is not the first time you will have received this message to be set apart. God has already been speaking to you in various ways and at different times. Some of you may even feel in your hearts that time is running out for you. You know that you either have to obey God or face the consequences. Other readers are receiving this message for the very first time and you are gulping everything down. You are hungry. You have been asking questions and now you are saying, 'Maybe this is the answer.' You are eager to get started on the journey. Then there are others who are saying, 'Mmm, God has given that guy John a nice message but I am not ready right now to take up something this serious.'

Whichever category you may fall in, I plead with you in the name of the Lord not to miss the timing of God. Moving in the Lord's timing is a major key to success. When we are operating in the timing of the Lord, things may be hard but the grace will be there. Do not miss what God is saying at this hour.

Identify the Idols in Your Life

I have shared with you how the Lord led me to make a list of the areas in my life in which I had not been giving my all to Him, and then another list of the reasons and excuses why I had not been doing so. I encourage everyone to do this. We have to identify and recognise the enemies in our life before we can fight them. We have to pinpoint the hidden hindrances embedded in our system. I believe this is the way to begin the journey of being set apart. The very words 'set apart' imply that there are things we need to be separated *from*. Those things have to be identified before the separation can occur.

It Takes God

As you sit down with the Lord to identify the hindrances to your walk with God, you will be overwhelmed by how disobedient you have been and also by the realisation that on your own you cannot possibly cut yourself loose from all the numerous chains binding you. You will find that while deep in your heart you are longing to be free, in your flesh, in your emotions, everything will be crying out against change of any description. A bitter struggle will begin.

Having taken the first step of identifying your enemies, step number two is to recognise that on your own you cannot overcome them all. Most of us know how many times we have tried to seek God but then we got tired and abandoned everything. There is a very real and strong opposition to any attempt to advance spiritually.

So what shall we do? We want to change but find ourselves unable to get very far on our own. What is the answer to this dilemma? The answer is God! Only God can give us real and lasting breakthrough. Only God can help us. It takes God and only God.

Beloved, the answer is *not* to focus on our bondages and limitations. Yes, we need to recognise them but we cannot eliminate them on our own. There is only one Person who can. His name is Jesus.

End of Yourself

But the Lord cannot help us unless we have reached the point of surrender, the point where we are genuinely able to say, 'Lord, I have come to the end of myself. I have been trying to fool people into believing that I am OK, but now I have come to accept that I am no good on my own. I surrender. Come and help me or I will die.' Beloved, the day you acknowledge that you cannot do it all by yourself anymore, will be the best day of your life. Because you see, God starts where we end. When you don't know what to do anymore, when you lay it all on the altar, when you are just about ready to give it all up, if you will allow it, that is when the Lord will show up. If right now you are at that point of surrender, don't be discouraged. Instead, thank God that you have at last come to the place where you can be helped.

It takes time to come to that point of surrender. Human pride doesn't want to admit defeat. That is why people struggle so much. We struggle to overcome sin, to serve God, to do good, etc. The more we struggle, the more we fail, but we still insist on going on in our own way. But beloved, it doesn't work that way. We will not see what God can do until we fully surrender.

Never Too Late

Jeremiah 29:11 tells us that it is not God's plan that we should fail: He wants to give us hope and bring us to the place where we can see our desires come to pass. We may not be where God wants us to be right now but He doesn't run away from us. He is always nearby, waiting for us to turn around so that He can direct us to that place in which He desires to see us. Unfortunately, often when we realise that God is waiting for us to turn around, we instead go even further away from Him. We may even go as far as stopping attending church, etc., but the Lord is always thinking of how to get us back to the desired place.

God's heart cries out for salvation, not destruction. John 10:10 says that the devil comes to steal, kill and destroy, but the Lord came that we might have life in abundance. No matter how far we have drifted away, with God we can always begin again. Ezekiel 18:21 promises that God will forgive anyone who repents regardless of how sinful they might have become. Yes, a prophet may even have pronounced judgement on us, but if we decide to repent and call upon God for mercy, He will have mercy.

Beloved, God is for us. God is willing to help us. We must grasp hold of this anchor. God's Word says,

> *'A broken and a contrite heart –*
> *These, O God, You will not despise.'* (Psalm 51:17)

If you do not believe that God loves you and is eager to work with you so that you can be restored, you will keep trying to help yourself, which is of course a futile business. Hebrews 4:15–16 says,

*'For we do not have a High Priest who cannot sympathize with
our weaknesses, but was in all points tempted as we are, yet
without sin. Let us therefore come boldly to the throne of grace,
that we may obtain mercy and find grace to help in time of
need.'*

The Lord Jesus, our High Priest, understands our weaknesses.
He knows our failures so well. He Himself struggled with
the same temptations as we do, but, unlike us, He overcame.
Because He overcame, we can depend on Him to help us overcome too. We need to go to Him and say, 'Lord, I do not like
what I have discovered about my life. I thought I was OK
but now I see how so far away from Your standard I am. You
have brought me this far but now, Lord, I need Your help. I
sin easily. My world rules my life. Satan's works against and
through me are biting hard. I cannot go on this way. I need
help and only You can do it.'

Build New Foundations

Beloved, the journey of being set apart is possible only as we
begin to make God our total focus; only as we allow God
Himself to become, not just in word but also in reality, the
foundation of our lives. If God is going to help us, and if
our sole purpose in life is to be set apart for Him, then our
relationship with God must be the focal point of our lives.

We have to renew and strengthen that relationship to the
extent where God can easily reach us and break open our
prison gates. Everything else must become secondary. We
have to seek God with all of our hearts.

The Passion of the Apostle Paul

In Philippians 3, Paul the apostle admits that he reached a
point in his life when everything else seemed like rubbish
compared to his passion to win and know Christ. In the
natural Paul had an impressive background. So religious had

he been that he dared write that, as far as the law was concerned, he had been blameless (v. 6). A Hebrew of Hebrews, a
leading Pharisee, a true Israelite – all these were Paul's
credentials; but a time came when he put aside everything so
that he could follow after Christ without any distraction or
baggage.

> *'But what things were gain to me, these I have counted loss for
> Christ. Yet indeed I also count all things loss for the excellence
> of the knowledge of Christ Jesus my Lord, for whom I have
> suffered the loss of all things, and count them as rubbish, that
> I may gain Christ and be found in Him, not having my own
> righteousness, which is from the law, but that which is through
> faith in Christ, the righteousness which is from God by faith.'*
> (verses 7–9)

Paul was saying that he could no longer engage in his religious
efforts because their effect was negative: he would have been
making a loss; he would have missed the real thing. What
he needed was Christ, not his efforts at trying to attain his
own righteousness. Through experience, Paul had come to
know that all his works of righteousness were like filthy rags
to God. He now knew that only the righteousness provided by
faith in Christ could avail. Paul had grown tired of his own
efforts at keeping the Ten Commandments, and he wanted to
get hold of the One who could make him truly righteous.

Paul was talking first about the old life he had led before
coming to Christ, then about his new life in the Lord and,
finally, about the life after sanctification to the Lord when he
was ready to give up everything for the sake of his walk with
God. At the time he wrote the letter to the Philippians, Paul
was a Christian, an apostle with signs following his ministry, a
seasoned missionary who had travelled the nations planting
churches, etc., but he was still not all that he desired to be in
God. Towards the end of his ministry, he wrote a letter to the
Romans, lamenting that he was in a battle in which he did not
always do what he knew to be right. His inner man loved God

but in his outer man, in the flesh, there was another law that forced him to live contrary to his desire. There was something within him that kept drawing him away from the right actions, and limiting him in his walk with God. There was sin in him.

An apostle, a church planter, a great minister, and yet he recognised what many do not want to today: that there was a power operating within him that worked counter to his faith, holding him back, diverting him, distracting him, hindering him. This great apostle said, '*Oh, wretched man that I am. Who will deliver me . . . ?*' In other words, 'I recognise that I am in bondage. My life is not totally free. I need deliverance.' But thank God, he recognised too that there was a solution: through the Lord Jesus Christ (Romans 7:24–25).

In Philippians 3:10, Paul wrote that he had one mission in his life: to know Christ. He said he wanted to know Jesus in His power. He wanted the deepest fellowship possible with the One who had given up everything so that He could have Paul. He was even willing to die, in whatever way, so that he could be assured of his place among those who will be resurrected.

Paul reached a point at which he did not focus on anything else – not on big ministry, prosperity, fame – but only on GOD. Paul's cry was, 'Lord, if you do not help me, I am finished.' Beloved, you can choose to continue struggling with life on your own if you want to, but I guarantee all you will get is defeat and disappointment. Or you can decide to seek the only One who can work within you, change you and complete the work of setting you apart. Which one will you choose: struggle or surrender? The journey begins with surrender.

Personal Testimony

Before I came to the Lord, my life was one big mess. I was working for a company but things weren't moving. I had no money and I was sick with a bad stomach ulcer and a painful chest ailment that doctors failed to diagnose. My people said it had to do with an ancestral spirit.

Then one day I read a book by Dennis Bennett entitled *Nine O'clock in the Morning*,[1] in which there were testimonies of how people had been filled with the Holy Spirit and had spoken in tongues. I was challenged. In my Roman Catholic religion, I had not heard about anyone having such an experience. I developed a longing to be filled with the Holy Spirit too. I asked one of my sisters if she knew anything about being filled with the Holy Spirit and if she had heard of anywhere where people had such experiences. When she mentioned the name of a prominent Pentecostal preacher whose name I knew, I promptly backtracked – I had been told the man was a false prophet! Then she said I could go to a lunch-hour fellowship led by Pastor Robert Kayanja somewhere on Luwum Street in Kampala.

For some time, I skipped lunch and went to the fellowship but I didn't see anyone get filled with the Holy Spirit. Sometimes the people sang and looked to heaven with smiling faces, making me wonder whether they were getting the Holy Spirit when they did that.

Then one Monday, the preacher said that within seven days God would give us whatever we might ask for. I thought of what I could ask for: Help with my finances? Healing? What? Finally, I decided I would ask for the Holy Spirit. As I was just beginning to pray, I remembered that someone had preached that no one could get the Holy Spirit who wasn't saved. Well, that meant I had to quit my Roman Catholic religion. There was a struggle within me. Eventually, I prayed asking God to save me within the seven days or else I would know the preacher was a liar.

The following day, I met a pastor and asked him about being filled with the Holy Spirit. The pastor quoted many scriptures, most of which I knew because by that time I had already read the Bible through sixteen times, even though I wasn't saved. My major interest was speaking in tongues, and I asked the pastor to speak in tongues so that I could hear him. Well, at the end of it all, the pastor led me in a prayer of confession to receive Christ. He almost forced me to do it because I really didn't want to. After the prayer, I felt nothing at all – no joy, no warmth – therefore I concluded that I hadn't got saved yet.

After that I went to my office and the moment I sat down, an audible voice spoke to me telling me that I needed to believe that I was saved. The voice kept speaking in intervals for the next two days. Finally, I said, 'OK, I accept that I am saved. But Lord, I will wait for eight months before I make a full commitment because I want first to check to see if it really works.' That was Thursday. On Saturday, I backslid. I didn't want anything to do with being saved. Then, on Sunday, a young girl persuaded me to go to church with her. The sermon was on giving, which made me re-affirm that I wasn't ever going to get messed up with saved folk because they were all in it for the money.

After the service, I saw a girl whom I knew and, as we talked, she testified to me how she had been saved, filled with the Holy Spirit and had even prayed for sick people who had been healed. She punctuated her testimony with tongues. When I heard her speak in tongues, I told God, 'Lord, now I am saved with no conditions.'

Things started happening in my life rapidly after that. I was healed of the diseases I had. Two weeks after my conversion, I was filled with the Holy Spirit. One month later, I started preaching. Two months later, I opened up a fellowship. That second month I also took my first seven-day fast. From then on, I fasted for a week every month. By the end of the year, I was in full-time ministry.

The point of this testimony is that when we surrender to the Lord, things work themselves out. I wanted many things. I had many problems, all of which I had failed to find solutions for. But when I surrendered to the Lord, He came into my life, healed me, re-organised me and established me in His plans for my life. *He* is the answer.

Note
1. Dennis Bennett, *Nine O'clock in the Morning* (Kingsway, 1974).

Chapter 9

Redeeming the Time

In the previous chapter, I emphasised the truth that if we are going to be set apart for God, if we are going to make changes in our lives, if we are going to get to where we want to be in our walk with God, it will not happen through human struggle. The flesh profits nothing (John 6:63). The only way we are going to get to the place we desire in our hearts so much to be is by the Almighty God Himself taking us there.

However, we have a role to play too. While it is true that only the power of God can effect changes in our lives, we also have to co-operate with the Lord. We have to give Him room to operate in us. We have to choose to make Him the focus of our lives, and then take steps which will give Him the freedom to work within us. We have to draw close to Him, by making the choice and commitment to do the things that He shows us.

Get Your Priorities Right

Matthew 13:44 says that the kingdom of God can be likened to a man who, after finding a treasure hidden in a field, sells all that he has so that he can buy that field. The treasure becomes the priority and everything else becomes secondary.

As I mentioned in the previous chapter, once you discover the One who alone can change your life, it is only logical that you drop everything else and go after Him. Seeking God must be our first priority. God must come first, and then the other things can find their place around Him. We have to re-arrange our lives.

I am not saying that we should give up our jobs or marriages or anything like that, but that these areas of our lives, important as they are, must not crowd God out. Every single day of our lives, we must give time to being with the Lord.

This sounds so obvious, but all of us know that not many Christians give first priority to God in their daily routine. They allow just about anything to make them suspend the time they have set aside for being with the Lord. But beloved, if we keep letting other things crowd out our time for God, how is He going to help us? This journey of being set apart demands that we cut out of our lives anything that pulls us back from giving enough time to the Lord.

People who attend our annual AfriCamp conference often say when they get back home, 'We enjoy the conference so much, the time of prayer, worshipping God ... but when we get back home, we get really busy. There is no time for prayer, no time to be with God as we would like.' This is particularly true of our friends from the developed nations. And sure enough, when you examine their lifestyles, you can't help but agree with them. People work hard over long hours. I understand that. And even here in Africa, people can be so busy that they hardly find time for God. When they wake up in the morning there is just enough time to get ready for work. Back home in the evening, they are genuinely tired and they have just a little time to say a prayer and get to bed. And so people spend days without reading Scripture or even just communing with the Holy Spirit.

But the question I cannot help asking is: Why do some people find time for God while others do not? Everyone has twenty-four hours. I think it is a matter of priority. When something is a priority, we give it time. We may have all our wonderful excuses but the major reason for not seeking God is because we don't make seeking Him a priority, and the reason for this is because we don't know who we really are.

Jesus warned us to take care that our hearts are not over-burdened with greed and the worries of this daily life. Everyone is working so hard to get on in life, to provide for their needs and wants, and that is fine, but Jesus is saying, 'Hey! Take care. Don't let that consume all your life.' I look around and it is obvious that not many Christians take heed of Jesus' warning. Our jobs, families and our plans come first. They all have a place in our programme. But not God. Why? *Because He is not a priority.* We really don't see Him as essential to our well-being, even though we say He is.

It is like a student preparing for an exam. As the time for the exam draws close, he cannot continue as usual. He has to cut out non-essentials from his schedule so that he can concentrate on his books. He cuts out extra-curricular activities, limits conversations that won't help him, and cuts down on the number of hours he sleeps. Why? Because he is determined to get his degree. It is a priority for him. He doesn't need anybody to sit him down and teach him how to prioritise. He just knows! He can no longer afford to spare the time for sport, parties and spending long hours in conversation, etc. He guards his time so that he can study. That is how people pass their exams. It is the same principle in the kingdom.

Change your priorities. Drastic action is called for, and that is the only way to get started on this new walk. Don't start by working on your sins. Change your priorities and give God His time in your schedule, His quality time in your day, your week and your month.

Plan and Guard Your Time

The Lord said to me once: 'What you permit into your time, you are permitting into your life, and what you permit into your life, is what you become.'

It has been said that 'time is money', but with the understanding I now have, I say that *time is life*. After all, the length of our lives on earth is measured in terms of time. If a person spends a short time on earth, people speak of his/her life as being short. When someone dies, they say he/she was born on such and such a date and died on such and such a date.

What we allow to take our time becomes the seeds we sow into our lives. If I spend time watching dirty movies, I am sowing into my life stuff that will eventually make me dirty. If I spend time gossiping, I will harvest a lifestyle of gossip and slander. Whatever we spend our time on, we are allowing that thing to influence our lives. The way we use our time is very important.

Back in 1988, the Lord gave us this instruction: 'Every day, set your priority and bring it before Me. Then order the rest of your day around that priority. Make a programme for your day and stick to it. Do not drift through life aimlessly. Do not just react to situations. Face every day with a plan. Do not be idle.' At the time, it sounded like a good piece of advice but we didn't take it seriously. We knew that white people were the ones who were obsessed with that kind of thing. Now, I know better.

We need to start each day with prayer, seeking God for our programme for the day. In that way, we make God our priority and then build the rest of the areas of our lives around Him. When we thus plan our day with the Lord, we tune ourselves so that we hear the voice of the Holy Spirit more easily.

Beloved, we need to come to God afresh, empty. We need to empty our lives of both the good things and the bad things. We need to put everything on the altar. We should bring the twenty-four hours of our day to the Lord empty of pro-grammes. We come with our blank day and say, 'Lord, what are the things that will deepen my relationship with You, the things that will make me live my life in line with Your purposes? Show them to me so that I can make time for them in my mornings, afternoons and evenings. After I have fixed them in my day, I will then put in other essentials like work and relationships.'

Ask the Father, 'Lord, how do You want me to spend this week?' Not all the days will be the same. Ask Him how much of your time He wants to have each week, and plan to give

Him that time. After that put in the other important things, and then see about the less important ones. If there is no time left for something, give it up. You don't need it. Beloved, that is the cost of loving God. If the way I spend my day, week and month change, soon my year will change and then my life will change.

I am not advocating stopping everything and spending all your life in a prayer closet. What I am emphasising is letting God take first priority in your time. You can be sure that, once you start on this journey, every single day there will be someone or something that will try to disrupt your plan. There is nothing as difficult as starting on a new course when you are comfortable in the old one. You may consider your day planned and approved by God, and you begin to walk accordingly. But when the time for prayer comes, you realise that there is a football match on television and it is a second-round match. There will be the temptation to say, 'Oh no! God, I will pray after the soccer match.' If you give in to that, however, by the time the soccer match is over, you may be too tired to pray or, if your team has been defeated, you may feel in no mood to express your love to God. Distractions! There will always be something to divert you from your plan.

If you have planned your day with the Lord and you are determined to keep to it, when a disruption comes, the Lord will immediately speak to you through the inner witness as to whether He is the One changing your plan or whether it is the devil, or even your flesh. Planning your time makes you more sensitive to the Holy Spirit.

The plan you make with the Lord has to be guarded. And I am not just referring to sticking to the time you have set for prayer or studying the Word. It could be the time allotted to cooking that is being threatened with disruption. Maybe a friend drops by and asks you to accompany him or her somewhere, when you had planned to be in the kitchen. If you give in, by the time you get back to cooking, your entire schedule for the day will have been messed up and you will be forced to cut out some of the things you had planned. And usually the devil will tell you it is prayer or reading the Word that should go.

We Africans are not used to the kind of disciplined lifestyle I am talking about here, but let me remind all of us that redeeming the time is a command for all Christians, not just for white Christians. One of the reasons why we aren't where we are supposed to be with God is because we don't use our time wisely. We spend time on things that push us away from the Lord instead of on the things that bring us close to Him.

Identify Distractions and Fight Them

Every time you are distracted from doing what God wants, stop and ask yourself, 'What has distracted me? What has stopped me from living my life with God as priority and why does it have this kind of influence on me? Why does it have the power to turn me away from what I know is best for me?' When you dig down deep in that way, you begin to recognise an idol in your life, something that is more important to you than God.

Once you have pinned this idol down, there will be a fight within you as to whether to hold on to it or to let it go. One voice will tell you that *this is who you are*: it is what makes you you, and therefore you cannot part with it. If you are serious about the journey you are undertaking, do not listen. Now is the time to take that idol to the altar and nail it there. This is where travailing prayer comes in. You go to God and say, 'Lord, I admit that my heart is weak. My heart is running after something else. You know I am attracted to this idol more than You, but deliver me, O God. Lead me not into temptation, but deliver me from the evil one. Save me from those moments when I am tempted to give up my love for You and be captivated by this thing.' Then you begin to pray more specifically, 'Lord, save me from moments that try me beyond my capacity, and deliver me from the evil one.' Soon you will see the power of our Lord Jesus. God says, *'the one who comes to Me I will by no means cast out'* (John 6:37). He is faithful.

For instance, there will be times when you know you should be reading the Bible but you feel compelled to do something else. You ask, 'Why? What is diverting me?' If it is the enemy, the world or your weaknesses, you will recognise it. But you won't stop desiring it. The pressure will always be there. Then is the time to say in your heart, 'Lord, You know how much I want to go and do that – but I want to say I prefer You. I choose You above that. Meanwhile strengthen me, and help me overcome. Make me an overcomer.' God is faithful!

There will be other times when the Holy Spirit says to you, 'I want you to do this.' It may be prayer. If you are sensitive to distraction, you will ask, 'Why am I being compelled to change my plan?' As you examine the compulsion, the urge to change, you will realise that, in this case, it is God, not your flesh, or the world around you, or the devil. This is God. Then you can obey with the joy of knowing, 'I have heard the Lord'. As the voice of the Holy Spirit becomes more distinct, the guidance of God becomes clear and the joy of the Lord increases, and the joy of the Lord is our strength. People may not understand you, but there is a joy in hearing and doing. Not guessing. Even when it is painful, the pain is sweet. You may even have to give something up, but in your heart joy bubbles up, and when you come to worship and lift up your hands, the Holy Spirit is poured out, joy rises and you plunge into the presence. Your heart melts before God. Soon you realise, it is not by power or by might: it is the Holy Spirit making way for you step by step. You live one moment at a time. Why? Because you have already re-ordered your day and put Him first. When you put Him first He puts you first.

Chapter 10

True Worship

Nowadays praise and worship are being given prominence all over the world. There is much talk of intimacy, of falling in love with God – it has become fashionable. In terms of our journey to become set apart for God, true worship is our most important weapon.

Jesus told the Samaritan woman, whom He met at the well:

> *'But the hour is coming, and now is, when the true worshippers will worship the Father in spirit and truth; for the Father is seeking such to worship Him. God is Spirit, and those who worship Him must worship in spirit and truth.'*
>
> (John 4:23–24)

It is a fact that there is no shortage of worshippers, but it is vital to note that not all worship pleases the Father. He seeks those who will worship in spirit and in truth. God told the Jews through the prophet Isaiah:

> *'When you spread out your hands,*
> *I will hide My eyes from you;*
> *Even though you make many prayers,*
> *I will not hear.*
> *Your hands are full of blood.'*
>
> (Isaiah 1:15)

God was tired of empty worship without righteousness, purity and justice. Not all worship touches the Father's heart.

When we lift up our hearts and sing, 'I will serve no foreign God or any other treasure; You are my heart's desire, Spirit without measure . . . ',[1] do we really mean it? The implication of the song is that God is above all; there is nothing that compares to Him. In our spirit do we understand what we are singing? Yes, there are treasures, idols, that attract us and seek to take us away from the Lord, and in worship we fight them.

Gazing upon God

One definition of worship is 'gazing upon God'. When Moses gazed upon God, he returned a changed man, covered by the glory of the presence of God.

We all know that sometimes it is a struggle to get into that place of intimacy with God. We long to come into the presence and feel the Father, but it doesn't happen automatically. Well, gazing upon the Lord in worship is a quick way to enter the presence. As we gaze upon Him, admiring Him, offering ourselves to Him, telling Him how powerful and awesome He is, etc., our spirit begins to be moved. If we stay in that place long enough, expressing our adoration of Him in words or song, our spirit will soon know His presence in a very profound way.

The more we gaze upon Him, the more He reveals Himself: His love, power, goodness, majesty, etc. As our spirit and soul keep soaking up that revelation, we reach a point where we just want to bow before Him. We begin to see Him in His true light, as the greatest Being in the universe. We catch a revelation of His purity and, before long, our heart begins to remind us of the things that are holding us back from consecrating ourselves to Him. We are confronted with the reality of our idols and, very soon, we find that we cannot continue worshipping without first dealing with those idols.

This is where the battle begins to rage. We sense God asking us, 'Do you really mean it when you sing that you will serve no other God? What about all those idols blocking your clear view of Me?' We want to continue worshipping and enjoying

His presence, but our mind keeps going back to those areas of our life which we have not yielded totally. We realise that our heart loves something else more than Him. We are now faced with a decision: Do we cross that line and get the idol out of our life or do we cleave to it?

Holy Romance

Before the word 'intimacy' came to be popularly associated with worship, I used to tell people that worship is holy romance. True worship takes us to a place where we are deeply in love with God, not in the sense of 'feeling love' but because we catch the revelation of His great attributes and what He has done.

It is like family. We do not necessarily 'feel love' for our family, although feelings are of course there at times. When we are away from our family, we do not miss them because we feel love for them. We miss them because we remember them, wondering how they are and what they might be doing. We remember how they love us and the moments we have shared together in the past. Something in us begins longing to reach out to them. We remember our husband or wife, how he/she speaks, the things he/she likes doing, etc., and our heart wants to be with him/her. It is the same in worship. We love Him because of who He is, what He does and the way He ministers to us. We want to give Him the glory that He alone deserves.

Isaiah 42:5–8 is a good passage to use in worship. Every word that God says about Himself in this passage we can say back to Him in worship. At the end of the passage, He says that He gives His glory to no one else. He alone deserves the glory.

Covenant with God

As you gaze upon the Lord and romance with Him, you will be enabled to determine in your heart not to love or belong to anything or anyone else. You will be enabled to come into a covenant with God to belong to and love Him with all your heart. Because of your commitment, God will work with you through the entire process. He will put songs into your heart and, as you sing to Him, you will become aware of the depth of the bondage in which you were held. You will see how proud you have been, how great a hold money has had on you, etc. And with the revelation of the depth of the bondage will come the sincere desire and ability to repent.

God is not looking for perfect believers, preachers, etc., but for those who will exalt Him and worship Him in spirit and truth. If you make a covenant with God to exalt Him every day and give your life as a sacrifice, the Holy Spirit will keep directing you to the right paths as well as pointing out the things you get wrong. Worship is not just singing and speaking words of praise and adoration, it includes our entire walk with God. The heart can exalt God without even speaking a word.

I was once invited to speak at a small church. Throughout the time I was speaking, the pastor of that church kept softly interjecting with 'praise God' or 'amen'. At the time, I did not take much notice, but later the Holy Spirit prompted me and told me, 'Learn from him. He is a true worshipper.' The pastor wrote me a letter, and I noticed that whenever he referred to God, he used a capital 'H' for 'he' or 'him'. I noticed this because at first he had used a small 'h' and then he went over the letter again inserting a capital 'H'. Again the Spirit prompted me to learn from him. Even in his writing he worshipped God. He was poor and did not have much, but he worshipped God in his writing, speaking, listening, and in the common tasks of life.

We have got to covenant to be worshippers in spirit and truth. In all situations, let us exalt Him. When good things happen, we need to step back and exalt God. When bad things happen, we need to step back and exalt God.

Jesus taught us to pray by exalting the name of God, not only as we begin to pray but also as we end. That is how it should be in everything we do: we should start and end everything with worship. It is so simple but most people never do it. Nothing can replace the prayer of worship: it is the place where we see our flaws but they do not overwhelm us because at the same time we see the greatness of the Father and His ability to set us free.

Isaiah 40 says that those who wait on God will renew their strength. This is our God. Gaze into His glory. When we worship and exalt Him, everything else, including reason, melts away.

Covenant to worship God and exalt Him above every other thing, no matter how great it may be. Worship is an attitude that acknowledges that God is above the government, above circumstances and above people. It is only when we put Him in His rightful place that He is able to act. He says,

> *'And I, if I am lifted up from the earth, will draw all peoples to Myself.'*   (John 12:32)

He will fight our battles. True worship will raise us above all that binds and limits us and we will be set apart. Covenant today to be a seeker of God.

Note
1. From 'I lift my hands' by Andre Kempen, Kempen Music.

Chapter 11

A People of the Word

We are considering the practical steps that we are to take as we pursue the journey of being set apart. Remember, this isn't a one-off season of separation to seek God, but rather a lifestyle. It is a daily decision. It is a protracted war against the forces that seek to make us less than what God wants us to be.

We have talked about making the Lord the number one priority in our daily lives by planning our days around Him. In that way, we walk with Him throughout the day, conscious of His presence. In itself this will keep us from engaging in much of the stuff that pushes us away from pursuing the upward call in God.

Now, as we spend time seeking the Lord, one of the issues we have to settle is what it is that God wants us to be: what is His vision for our lives? Unless we have a clear understanding of God's plan and purpose for our lives, we cannot even begin to hope that we shall achieve our goal of being set apart from everything else, in order to realise that vision.

The next question is: how do we discover that plan and purpose? The answer is straightforward and simple: in the written Word of God! Do you want to find out what God's plan and purpose for your life is? Go back to the Word of God!

God's Purpose in Creating the Human Race

Many of us want to live for God, but we fail because we don't know who we are. There are so many voices that purport

to tell us who we are. Our society, our tribe and our education system have all labelled us, and we spend our lives
trying to live up to those labels. That is why so many people
are confused. If we really want to know who we are, there is
only one person to whom we should go: the Author of our
lives.

What did God make human beings for? Genesis 1:26 states
that purpose very explicitly:

> *'Then God said, "Let Us make man in Our image, according to
> Our likeness; let them have dominion over the fish of the sea,
> over the birds of the air, and over the cattle, over all the earth
> and over every creeping thing that creeps on the earth."'*

God created the human being so that He could have an agent
through whom to rule over the earth. Regardless of our
different giftings and callings, we are all here to exercise God's
kingdom rule on earth. Each man and woman is created to be
an agent of administering His kingdom on earth.

The Lord Jesus came to redeem fallen human beings, to stop
us being lost to the kingdom of God forever. He came preaching the gospel of the kingdom. When the disciples asked Him
to teach them how to pray, Jesus told them that they were to
pray that the kingdom of God would come and that His will
would be done on earth as in heaven.

When God says He wants us to be set apart for Him, He is
simply telling us to get back to the dream He had when He
created the human race. He created us to ensure that His
kingdom rule, power, attributes and authority are exercised
on earth just as they are in heaven. When we fail in this, we
cause God deep sorrow.

I may be emotionally deeply in love with God, I may
worship and sing and do all the right things, but if my life is
not causing the will of God to be implemented around me, I
am not living out my purpose for being on the earth. Being set
apart is all about the kingdom of God, about His will being
done on earth – in our families, communities, cities, nations –

as it is in heaven. You can't say that you love God but you want to have nothing to do with transformation. We are not here to protect our children and ourselves from the devil while caring nothing about what is going on around us. Our mission is, *'Go therefore and make disciples of all the nations'* (Matthew 28:19). We can't ignore it.

The Word as an Agent of Separation

John 1:1 says that the Word of God was there in the beginning and the Word is God. All things were created for Him and by Him. Hebrews 1:3 affirms that all creation is held in place by the Word of God's power. The Word of God is living and powerful, sharper than a double-edged sword, separating the spirit from the soul (Hebrews 4:12). Do you want to be set apart? The Word of God is the agent for separation.

What we do with the Word shows whether we love Jesus or not. John 14:21–24 says that if we love Him, we will obey His Word, and if we obey, Jesus and His Father will come and make their abode with us. The Lord promised that He would manifest Himself to those who were obedient to Him. What else do we desire more than that the Lord should make His abode with us, that the Lord should manifest Himself to us? His presence with us depends on how we handle His Word. And remember what 1 John 3:8 says: He was manifested to destroy the works of the devil. When the Lord manifests Himself to us, we are automatically separated from the works of the devil.

The God we serve is a big God but we can touch Him through His Word. That means in our seeking God, we must make the Word a priority. We must go back to the Word. Hebrews 1:3 says,

> *'The Son is the radiance of God's glory and the exact representation of his being, sustaining all things by his powerful word. After he had provided purification for sins, he sat down at the right hand of the Majesty in heaven.'*   (NIV)

All creation is held in place by the power of His Word. Get into the Word. It was there in the beginning, and when heaven and earth pass away, it will still be there. It is the power that cleanses. The Bible says that Christ cleanses the Church by the Word (Ephesians 5:26).

Beloved, it is time to get back into the Word. I want to give you five things to do with the Word:

- Read the Word daily
- Study the Word daily
- Pray the Word daily
- Obey the Word daily
- Speak the Word daily.

If we try to live by these five practices, our lives will never be the same again. The Word has power to create. It is like a seed. It fell into Mary's womb and created a baby. When it came to me, a sinner was delivered. When we speak it, demons flee. Give the Word its rightful position in your life.

As you immerse yourself in the Word, the Holy Spirit will come alongside you, teaching you many things and opening your eyes to the many truths in God's Word. He will teach you how to begin to hear Him and to learn how He speaks. As you yield yourself to Him and let Him guide you, He will teach you how to commune with Him and live with Him so that He can begin to work in your life changing you into the image and likeness of God. Then you will also begin to impact the world around you and the system that for so long you have been held captive by. This is just the beginning of the journey to be set apart for God. There is so much more to be discovered and the further you go, the more dependent you will become upon God. This journey to be set apart is a lifetime walk with God.

Chapter 12

Responding to the Call

I began this book by describing a worldwide Church struggling to make headway in a world in which satanic strongholds and world systems are becoming ever more deeply entrenched. I spoke of how the Lord had told me that following September 11, 2001 such a major shift had taken place in the heavenlies that only a people set apart for God would be able to overcome and make a difference in the societies in which we live. Through the course of this book I have described the journey we each need to undertake to be obedient to the Call of the Hour and now, as I conclude, I want to place before you a vision of the future that will be ours as we rise to the challenge of the true sons and daughters of our most glorious Father in heaven.

The Rising of a Set Apart People

I see scattered all over the world, often isolated and alone, men and women, young and old, people of every tribe and race, who are coming to the end of themselves. They are sick and tired of the way things are. Their hearts are revolting against the tide of the day, and deep within their spirits is a growing cry, **'Enough is enough!'**

They have had enough! They cannot take the status quo any more. Their hearts are crying out for the simplicity of the gospel. At the pain of losing everything they have lived for, they are turning their backs on the world and giving themselves to seeking the Lord with all their lives. They are rejecting the compromise and apostasy taught in our day and turning back to the age-old writings of the Bible to seek truth for themselves.

As they set themselves apart for the Lord, the Spirit of the Lord begins to draw near to them. They are still hidden as Daniel and his friends were in the three years of separation in Babylon (Daniel 1:3–20). But God is working within them to prepare them for the times ahead. Times of great trials and temptations! In the coming days many people will fall and betray their faith! No one will endure through the trials unless they are sustained by the Lord Himself. But those *'who know their God shall be strong, and shall carry out great exploits'* (Daniel 11:32).

I see small bands of men and women joining themselves to these individuals set apart for God. They are mentored and discipled by them, but this mentoring is not so much based on academic teaching and training, as on helping one another to connect up with God so deeply that God Himself will start to teach each individual directly (Jeremiah 31:33–34). The forerunners share their walk and encourage the others on, like iron sharpening iron, but every person has a direct encounter with God who teaches and deals with each individual divinely.

This is a very extraordinary company of men and women. They are committed to God and to each other in covenantal all-for-all love. None is considered greater than the other as they serve each other in humility, yet they all recognise the unique gifts and callings that God has given to each individual. They willingly make room for each person to fulfil the role God has so gifted them for. They celebrate their nothingness and prefer others above themselves in true Christlike lifestyle.

The Harvest

I see these small bands of men and women, young and old, determined to reach out to the lost and blind of the nations:

to break them free from the chains of bondage, the veil of deception, and the grip of the world. They immediately come under persecution and misrepresentation from both the public authorities of the day, and from many in the established Church. They go about in fear and trembling, yet they are willing to lay down their lives for the gospel and for the people they are called to serve.

But in spite of the perils to their lives, their work and ministry is powerful beyond comparison with anything that has ever been witnessed in the history of the modern Church. As they step out, mountains are levelled and valleys filled before them. Thousands of people across the continent who have sought the meaning of life in all kinds of perversions suddenly realise there is real meaning to life. The blind see, the sick are healed, the addicts set free, the prostitutes cleansed, and the proud humbled as the greedy abandon their worldly lusts and the prodigals rush home. The conventional churches can no longer hold the harvest so new structures are quickly coming into being which are free of unclean human control. The Church is finally changing to manifest the Lordship of our Jesus Christ.

The movement keeps growing and sweeping across cities and nations, until the kingdom of God is clearly visible. It is not a movement subject to the control of any one individual or organisation. Even those who were forerunners in it are swallowed up in its great surge and only God is seen to be going ahead of it (Joel 2:11).

Transformation

As the consecrated people penetrate the heavens with their travailing prayer, the clouds of darkness over whole communities begin to give way and open up to the flow of the Holy Spirit. Then it becomes clear that the system of the world is falling apart. Everything human beings have ever trusted in is giving way and, while some are struggling to survive in whatever way they can (becoming more and more wicked in the process), many more are finding hope and rest in the Lord. Communities begin to change, in all spheres of life.

The Church is being revived and transformed. Families are taking on a new form of stability and true love where all people feel safe and fulfilled. Public servants and political leaders are finding the meaning of truth, and this is beginning to have an effect on their service and on public institutions. The nations are being transformed: not by power or by might, but by the Holy Spirit.

This is happening at the same time as the forces of evil themselves are growing ever darker and more aggressive. No longer is it easy to be a Christian. Only those who are wholly sold out for Christ can stand up against the pressure and persecution. The battle of the ages is reaching its climax, and for all those who are set apart and prepared by Him it is a time of great victory.

This is the company of modern-day Nazarites: *set apart for God*, and committed to finishing the work of the Great Commission against all odds before the Day of His appearance. Their driving force is the battle cry of the Lord who is coming soon. Each one of them is looking forward to the day of His appearing, when we shall see Him as He is. Then we will gaze into His eyes, see that smile, and hear those precious words: 'Well done, faithful servant!' For this we give up everything so that we may know Him and the power of His resurrection (Philippians 3:7–12).

The Call

These words ring loud in my spirit: the process has already started! All across the nations are men and women who have heard the call of the Lord to be set apart. While many have chosen to procrastinate and rest in vain excuses, there are those who have already started the walk. They have counted the cost and concluded that God is worth more to them than the attractions of this present age. They would rather seek the abiding riches and fulfilment that is found only in Him who has been rejected and so misrepresented by His own Church in our day. God is already at work in these lives. They are hidden in His safe places – with all those that God is adding to them.

This is a vision of what is happening in the Spirit in our day. Those who have the Spirit of God and hunger for Him can see clearly what God is doing. The call to be set apart is not one to argue about. We must either respond 'Yes' or 'No'. We all know that human efforts have failed to solve the problems of our world, and we are in no doubt that, unless Jesus intervenes soon, we will no longer be able to recognise the biblical Church of our Lord in the modern Church.

The Lord will not force Himself on His people ... and neither will He come to us while we are stuck in our ways. He calls us to lay down our lives for His. The glory of God flows where the Christ life flows. This is the call of the hour: *set yourselves apart for the Lord*. He will work deeply in your life to prepare you for the times ahead. He will do in you what you cannot do for yourself and will bring you to the fulfilment of your destiny in the world.

> *'Blow the trumpet in Zion,*
> *And sound an alarm in My holy mountain!*
> *Let all the inhabitants of the land tremble;*
> *For the day of the LORD is coming,*
> *For it is at hand ... '*

(Joel 2:1)

Resources

The following workbooks and books written by John Mulinde are available from World Trumpet Mission to help those seeking to undertake the journey to be set apart for God:

Set Apart For God Workbook 1 – The Call
Set Apart For God Workbook 2 – The Nazirite Walk
Set Apart For God Workbook 3 – The Covenant Love of God

Transforming Your World
Pursuing God's Destiny
Healing the Wounded Spirit

For further information on the work of World Trumpet Mission, visit our web site:

www.worldtrumpetmission.org

or send enquiries to:

World Trumpet Mission – Africa
Trumpet Media
PO Box 8085, Kampala
Uganda
email: trumpet@infocom.co.ug

World Trumpet Mission – UK
Christian Life Centre
12 St James Road
Hereford HR1 2QS
England
email: info@trumpetmission.org.uk

World Trumpet Mission – USA
Hunters Creek Community Church
123 Hand Street
Kissimmee, Florida 34741
United States of America